NEW TESTAMENT PROBLEMS

NEW TESTAMENT PROBLEMS

by

T. FAHY, M.A.

Regius Professor of Ancient Classics, University College, Galway;
sometime
Professor of Ancient Classics, St. Patrick's College, Maynooth

DUBLIN
CLONMORE AND REYNOLDS LTD
LONDON
BURNS AND OATES LTD

First Printed 1963

225
FAHY.
461320.

MADE AND PRINTED IN THE REPUBLIC OF
IRELAND BY CAHILL AND CO., LTD.,
DUBLIN FOR CLONMORE AND REYNOLDS LTD.
NIHIL OBSTAT : DIONYSIUS Ó H-EIDHIN,
CENSOR DEPUTATUS. DIE 16 AUGUSTI, 1960.
IMPRIMI POTEST : ✠MICHAEL, EPUS
GALVIENSIS ET DUACENSIS. 17 AUGUSTI, 1960.

In like manner, therefore, ought we to explain the original text, which having been written by the inspired author himself, has more authority and greater weight than any, even the very best translation. . . .

And if the wished for solution be slow in coming or does not satisfy us, . . . let us not wax impatient thereat, seeing that in us also is rightly verified what the Fathers and especially Augustine, observed in their time, viz.: God wished difficulties to be scattered through the Sacred Books inspired by him, in order that we might be urged to read and scrutinise them more intently, and experiencing in a salutary manner our own limitations, we might be exercised in due submission of mind.

Extracts from the Encyclical Letter of
Pope Pius XII *Divino Afflante Spiritu.*

Foreword

MONSIGNOR FAHY has devoted his life to teaching the classics in Maynooth and University College, Galway. Now that he has retired from teaching he is applying his knowledge of Greek to the elucidation of questions in the Septuagint and the New Testament. All will agree that classical scholarship is a fundamental prerequisite for the understanding of these texts. Monsignor Fahy has collected a number of essays on Biblical problems in this book where he applies his great knowledge of Greek, with remarkable effect in my humble opinion. Whether experts agree with him or not, all must rejoice at seeing him devote his ripe and wide scholarship to the fuller understanding of the Word of God.

That is a work to which the Popes have invited Catholic scholars in the last fifty years. It is a labour that brings great honour and merit to a scholar and to a priest.

In offering my congratulations to Monsignor Fahy, I cannot help quoting the words which St. Jerome, the prince of biblical scholars, wrote in that letter to Nepotian which we read in the 2nd nocturn of matins of the 7th Sunday after Pentecost, "Senectus eorum qui adolescentiam suam honestis artibus instruxerunt et in lege Domini meditati sunt die et nocte, aetate fit doctior, usu tritior, processu temporis sapientior, et veterum studiorum dulcissimos fructus metit".

✠MICHAEL,
Bishop of Galway.

MOUNT SAINT MARY'S,
    GALWAY.
        14th August, 1960.

Contents

Chapter One

THE MARRIAGE OF OUR LADY AND ST. JOSEPH

(St. Luke 1 : 26 ff. ; St. Matthew 1 : 18 ff.)

THE traditional view seems to be that Our Lady and St. Joseph were formally married only after her return from the visit to St. Elizabeth some three months after the Annunciation. Then for the first time, it is claimed, she came to live in the home of St. Joseph and became his wife legally, having lived previously in the home of her parents as the betrothed of St. Joseph. Those who hold this view do not put forward any theory as to where the Annunciation took place, but it would seem reasonable to infer that the home of Mary's parents was the scene of the events of the Annunciation.

Traditionalists, as we shall call them for convenience, point out that espousals were a binding contract even though months or years elapsed before the man claimed his bride in marriage. But, even though the betrothed maiden could during this time be spoken of as the wife of her fiancé, marital relations were forbidden and looked upon not only as "improper and indecent but as disgraceful and sinful." It is claimed that espousals, like marriage, could be ended only by a bill of divorce.

It seems to me that the Gospel narrative becomes more intelligible and that the position of the Holy Family before and even after the Nativity is more correctly defined on the basis that Our Lady and St. Joseph had been united in virginal marriage before the date of the Annunciation, and had been living together in the home of St. Joseph, where, in all probability, the Annunciation took place. In fact, I venture to say that there is

11

no foundation for the traditional view beyond the misinterpretation of the word ἐμνηστευμένη and perhaps a reluctance to associate Our Lady's name with marriage until after the conception of her Son. Is it to be understood that the betrothal of Mary and Joseph was, in the first instance, preliminary to ordinary marriage and that the intervention of the Annunciation altered matters? The status of betrothal did not enjoy the privileges claimed for it. Betrothal, being only a step in preparation for marriage, did not confer the dignity of marriage and falls far short of virginal marriage in giving due honour to the Mother of God.

The evidence of the gospels: St. Luke

Let us examine the evidence of the Gospels, scanty but sufficient to establish the thesis that before the Annunciation Mary and Joseph were united legally and formally in virginal marriage.

St. Luke (1 : 27 ff.) tells us that *the Angel Gabriel was sent from God to a city in Galilee named Nazareth to a virgin espoused to a man named Joseph.* The word *espoused* (ἐμνηστευμένη) should be interpreted here in the sense not of "betrothed" or "engaged" but "married." This is certainly the meaning of the word in the next chapter; and no author, least of all a stylist such as St. Luke, is likely to use the same word, and that too a key word, in different senses in immediately successive chapters. In 2 : 5 St. Luke says that *St. Joseph went up from Nazareth to Bethlehem to enrol with Mary, his espoused, who was with child* (τῇ ἐμνηστευμένῃ αὐτῷ). Now, all commentators concede that at this particular time, immediately before the Nativity, Our Lady and St. Joseph were legally married. Mary was Joseph's wife and registered as such in the census records. The word used by St. Luke, to describe the status of Mary, is ἐμνηστευμένη and the meaning, "his virgin wife." It will be noted that St. Luke does not deem it necessary to add the word γυναικί. In Greek literature μνηστεύειν signifies "to woo or win a bride," whereas γαμεῖν connotes marital relations in marriage. From other contexts it is clear that St. Luke, and St. Matthew also, fully appreciated the distinction between the two words (St. Luke 16 : 18 ; St. Matt. 19 : 9). In St. Luke 2 : 5 then, beyond a shadow of doubt, ἐμνηστευμένη signifies a legally wedded wife, not merely a betrothed. The presumption that the word has the same meaning in 1 : 27 is so strong as to amount to a certainty. And it can be safely assumed that the same word when used exactly in the same context by St. Matthew, has the same meaning as St. Luke attaches to it.

The reply of Our Lady to the Angel on the occasion of the Annunciation, leads to the same conclusion, namely, that by this time she and St. Joseph had been united in virginal marriage. When the Angel announced to Mary that she would *conceive in her womb and bear a child*, she replied *how can this be since I know not man?* Now, carnal knowledge outside of marriage was contrary to the moral law and considered particularly heinous in the case of betrothed virgins. Stoning to death was the penalty prescribed for convicted guilt (Deut. 22 : 21). Our Lady's statement, therefore, cannot be interpreted as meaning that she had avoided something sinful in itself. Her meaning, rather, was that though married she had renounced the privileges of marriage that lead to motherhood, and this implied a compact with her husband. If Mary was unmarried and had taken a vow of virginity, she could be released from it by her own consent. If her husband was party to such a vow, her consent alone would not be sufficient for release from it. Our Lady's statement to the Angel must be interpreted as meaning that she is not free to consent to motherhood in the ordinary way. It was only when she was assured by the Angel that her motherhood would be supernatural through the direct intervention of the Holy Spirit, that she consented: *The Holy Spirit shall come upon thee and the power of the most High shall overshadow thee. Wherefore also that which is conceived shall be called holy, [being] the Son of God* (St. Luke 1 : 35).[1]

Shortly after the Annunciation, Our Lady set out for the home of St. Elizabeth, whose name had been mentioned by the Angel. According to the traditional view Mary set out from the house of her parents, under whose jurisdiction she was still living as merely betrothed. In the opinion being put forward here, she set out from the home of St. Joseph, her legal husband. It is quite clear from the subsequent account that she had not informed St. Joseph of the events of the Annunciation. This was a secret reserved by God himself for communication to those specially favoured. St. Elizabeth, *filled by the Holy Spirit*, saluted her as *the Mother of my Lord* (Lk. 1 : 42–3). St. Joseph was to be afterwards informed by a special messenger from God. Mary spent

---

[1]The subject here is τὸ γεννώμενον and ἅγιον is predicate. The Vulg. version differs from the Greek.

about three months with Elizabeth and then returned *to her own house* (Lk. 1 : 56). That is, she did not return to the home of St. Joseph but to the home of her parents. That this is not an unwarranted assumption I hope to show afterwards. At this stage St. Matthew takes up the narrative.

St. Matthew

The genealogy of Christ was as follows: His Mother Mary was espoused to Joseph (Mt. 1 : 18). *Espoused* ($\mu\nu\eta\sigma\tau\epsilon\upsilon\theta\epsilon\acute{\iota}\sigma\eta\varsigma$) here has the same meaning as in St. Luke 2 : 5 and 1 : 27. The word *mother* presupposes family life with her husband St. Joseph, and could not be associated in the public mind with mere betrothal. The following words $\pi\rho\grave{\iota}\nu \ \sigma\upsilon\nu\epsilon\lambda\theta\epsilon\~\iota\delta \ a\grave{\upsilon}\tau o\acute{\upsilon}\varsigma$ indicate that the union was virginal: *without intercourse on their part she was found with child of the Holy Spirit.* (Mt. 1 : 18). The word $\pi\rho\acute{\iota}\nu$ quite regularly refers to an event that did not occur, and should not be translated "before," which has implications not contained in the Greek word. Traditionalists interpret $\pi\rho\grave{\iota}\nu \ \sigma\upsilon\nu\epsilon\lambda\theta\epsilon\~\iota\nu \ a\grave{\upsilon}\tau o\acute{\upsilon}\varsigma$, as meaning before Mary and Joseph came to live together in the home of St. Joseph. $\sigma\upsilon\nu\epsilon\lambda\theta\epsilon\~\iota\delta$ has a recognised connotation of marital intercourse and the context here clearly indicates that such is the meaning. Intercourse was lawful only for husband and wife, not for parties merely betrothed. The form of expression here indicates that the Evangelist presupposed the lawfulness of such relations, admissible only if Mary and Joseph were united in marriage.

The next verse (19) is one of particular importance and must be examined in detail: *Joseph her husband being a just man and not wishing to expose her, decided to divorce her secretly* ('Iωσήφ δὲ ὁ ἀνὴρ αὐτῆς δίκαιος ὢν καὶ μὴ θέλων αὐτὴν δειχματίσαι ἐβουλήθη λάθρα ἀπολῦσαι αὐτήν). After Mary's return to Nazareth from the home of Elizabeth, Joseph discovered what appeared to him to be certain evidence of her unfaithfulness, conscious as he was that he had fulfilled his pact of virginity. The Evangelist tells us that Joseph was a just man and not wishing to expose his wife to public opprobrium, that he planned a certain course of action. It is wrong to suggest, as the traditional interpretation claims, that Joseph's justice consisted in not wishing to expose his wife to opprobrium. His justice consisted in his determination to fulfil the law. Let us see what courses were open to St. Joseph, what course he planned to take and the reason why. We shall proceed first on the assumption that Mary and Joseph were not formally married, only betrothed.

Unfaithfulness in betrothal

The case, then, is that the man has discovered unfaithfulness in his betrothed, and charges that before her marriage her virginity has been violated. The case is fully dealt with in Deuteronomy 22 : 14 ff. The charge against the betrothed is brought to the notice of the parents. The parents in turn, bring the matter before the village court, "the ancients at the gate." Note that there is no obligation on the man to lay the matter before the village court. That is the business of the parents. And it can be safely presumed that the parents would be slow to take action unless convinced of the justice of their case and their capability to prove it. Death by stoning in public was the penalty if the girl was found guilty (Deut. 22 : 21). Note that there is no question here of the man instituting proceedings for divorce. This course of procedure would have exactly suited Joseph. He would be fulfilling the law in referring the matter to Mary's parents, and the sequel would rest with them. They were not likely to expose their child to public opprobrium, and in any event St. Joseph would be absolved from further responsibility once he had referred the case to Mary's parents, who could be trusted to treat their child with the utmost consideration. Joseph did not plan to adopt this course, because it was not open to him. Mary was his wife before the law, not his betrothed, and the case was covered by a different statute:

Unfaithfulness in marriage

If a man take a wife and have her and she find not favour in his eyes for some uncleanness, he shall write a bill of divorce, and shall give it in her hand, and send her out of his house (Deut. 24 : 1).

His conscience, therefore, impelled Joseph, *being a just man*, to obey this law. His affection and respect for his wife prompted him to save her public reputation. How were these attitudes reconcilable? Joseph planned to divorce her secretly ($\lambda\acute{a}'\theta\rho\alpha$). How was this possible in the circumstances, seeing that she had to be handed a bill of divorce and put away from his house? There was no publicity involved in a bill of divorce. The odious publicity was evidently connected with putting the woman away from the home. The word δειχματίσαι means "to make a public show of." St. Joseph wished to avoid this and at the same time fulfil the law. Circumstances favoured him. Mary, realizing before her return from the home of Elizabeth that the signs of conception were now evident, and conscious that Joseph knew nothing of the events of the Annunciation, decided to return *to her own house* in Nazareth (St. Luke 1 : 56), and not to the home of Joseph from which she set out. Joseph, discovering from his own observation or from the observation of others, what he was convinced was her unfaithfulness, refused *to take her over* (παραλαβεῖυ Mt. 1 : 20) to his home, knowing that the law would compel him to put her out, and he wished to save his wife this indignity. Joseph, therefore, by handing his wife a bill of divorce would fulfil the law. She had already left his house. He would thus divorce her secretly.

Commentators state that St. Joseph's justice (δίκαιος ὢν) consisted in refusing to expose his wife (betrothed) to the publicity of the village court. If the law enjoined such an obligation on Joseph, being *a just man* he would have fulfilled it, however repellent to his feelings the course might be. Let it be remembered that there was at no time an obligation on the aggrieved man to lay the case before the village court. That, as we have seen, was a matter for the parents of the accused girl. Let it be remembered also that the proceedings as described in Deuteronomy 22 : 14 ff. bear no relation to divorce. Joseph realized that the law compelled him to divorce his wife. He planned (ἐβουλήθη) to obey the law by divorcing her secretly.

Mary thy wife

When Joseph was deeply troubled by this matter an angel of the Lord appeared to him saying: *Joseph, son of David, fear not to take over* (παραλαβεῖν) *Mary thy wife. That which has been conceived in her is of the Holy Spirit* (Mt. 1 : 20). Joseph, through fear of having to expel her as enjoined by the law, had not taken over Mary to his home after her return from her visit to Elizabeth. He is now assured there is no reason to fear the law as the charge of unfaithfulness is without foundation. Traditionalists understand the angel's message as "Fear not to take over Mary thy betrothed as thy wife." What authority is there for interpreting τὴν γυναῖκά σου as "thy betrothed"? In China and India today, girls of tender age are spoken of as the "wives" of boys of equally tender age. Those who know them, know they are not wives but destined to be wives. It is a *modus loquendi* and nobody is deceived. The term, in other words, is explained in its context. Betrothal in ancient Israel defined the status of the girl and hedged her round with safeguards against the day of her marriage. But commentators exaggerate the significance of betrothal. It is claimed that a bill of divorce was required to dissolve betrothal just as in the case of marriage. What evidence is there for this claim? Where there is no marriage there is no divorce. It is claimed also that sin with a betrothed girl was adultery. Deuteronomy (22 : 22–4) draws a sharp distinction between sin with a betrothed and sin with "another man's wife." The sinners in the latter case are described as adulterers. Not so the former. Where in sacred Scripture is there authority for translating γυνή as "betrothed" not "wife"? I find only two instances in the Septuagint where γυνή means "betrothed" (Gen. 29 : 21 ; Deut. 22 : 24), and in each instance the context makes the sense as clear as noonday. There is no authority in the New Testament for interpreting γυνή as "betrothed." In the Apocalypse the Bride of the Lamb is called γυνή (19 : 7 ; 21 : 9). But this is mystical language, and again the context leaves no doubt about the sense. If γυναῖκα in St. Matthew 1 : 20 must be translated "betrothed," why not translate "Zachary and his betrothed Elizabeth" (Lk. 1 : 5), "Annanias with his betrothed Sapphira" (Acts 5 : 1)? The reply is that the context does not authorize it. Words have a definite meaning acquired by usage and convention, and this meaning must be retained unless the context gives a direction to the contrary. When the angel in his communication to Joseph describes Mary as his wife, we must accept it that Mary was Joseph's wife, and not his betrothed. To interpret γυναῖκα here as "betrothed" is to beg the whole question.

The viewpoint of propriety

There is a further argument *e rerum convenientia*, where the question is examined from the angle of common sense, from the viewpoint of ordinary propriety. The traditional claim is that Our Lady and St. Joseph were married only some three or four months after the Annunciation; that previously Mary was betrothed and lived with her parents; that now for the first time she comes to live in the home of St. Joseph. Marriage celebrations in Palestine were occasions of great festivity, we are told by commentators, sometimes lasting a whole week. The marriage feast at Cana is said to have been no exception in this respect. It is most probable also that the marriage of Mary and Joseph was no exception in the matter of festivity. Belonging as they both were to the royal house of David, they would be expected to honour the national traditions. Let us here reflect that the secret of the Annunciation had been religiously observed and that the marriage between Mary and Joseph would be regarded as just another marriage. Undoubtedly the remarkable sanctity of bride and bridegroom could not have escaped the notice of their neighbours, but this circumstance often serves only to whet the appetite of gossip. Nazareth, by modern standards, was only a village, and like every village we may presume Nazareth had its quota of gossips. Privacy has never been a feature of Eastern life. Even if there had been no festivities on the occasion of their marriage it would have been known to all her neighbours that it was then for the first time Mary came to live in the home of Joseph. The date of the Nativity was less than six months distant. It is unnecessary to enlarge on this aspect of the matter. Surely no whisper of irregularity could be associated with the life of the Holy Family that was destined to be the model of family life for all time.

Let us reflect also that Jesus had implacable enemies who were prepared to stoop to any depth to defame him and who would not shrink from any insult, founded though it was on idle gossip, that could be hurled against him or his parents. The position that Our Lady and St. Joseph were married only some months after the Annunciation is untenable from any point of view. It will not be claimed that their marriage took place during Mary's absence in the home of Elizabeth. The only position that squares with Scripture and common sense is that Our Lady and St. Joseph were united in virginal marriage before the date of the Annunciation. Joseph's reaction to the discovery of what appeared unfaithfulness in Mary on her return from the home of Elizabeth, is the strongest human testimony to the integrity of their virginal marriage. The testimony of the angel followed.

To show that the question is not one of mere academic import I shall quote a brief extract from an article by a writer whose *bona fides* is beyond question and who aims at reconciling with reality the Gospel narrative as traditionally interpreted: "So far the suggestion is that at the time of his marriage Joseph was anxiously exercised how to protect the good name of Mary and the baby she had three or four months earlier conceived, how therefore to take steps to conceal her condition from whoever knew the date of her marriage. The only way open to him was to move from Nazareth. The census decree was already promulgated. He intended to leave Nazareth, and he had to go to Bethlehem; so he would settle down there. As moreover he had to move quickly if his wife's secret was to be kept, he took her to Bethlehem almost at once after their marriage. St. Luke describes him as going with Mary who was espoused to him, 'she being with child'—and it is possible that just as the omission of the word 'wife' is a discreet reference to Mary's virginity, so the phrase 'she being with child' is a delicate and reticent allusion to Joseph's chief motive for leaving Nazareth and taking her with him."[1]

---

[1] Rev. Vincent Turner, S.J., *The Downside Review* (Winter 1947–8, p. 60).

Chapter Two

ST. PAUL'S ROMANS WERE JEWISH CONVERTS

It is generally admitted that St. Mark's Gospel was written for the gentile Christians of Rome, whom St. Peter had converted. The internal evidence points to this conclusion. The Gospel was written sometime in the decade A.D. 53-63. The Jewish population of Rome at that time has been estimated at 50,000, and it is most likely that there was a second Christian community, composed probably exclusively of Jews, also converted by St. Peter and his assistants.

It is difficult to understand St. Paul's Epistle to the Romans except on the assumption that it was written mainly for Jews. This letter has been assigned to the opening months of A.D. 58. The fact that St. Mark is "silent about the Mosaic Law and its relation to the New Testament economy"[1] would perhaps indicate that St. Paul's Epistle is prior in date to St. Mark's Gospel. St. Mark, realizing that this whole question had been amply treated by St. Paul, would not consider further discussion necessary, seeing that St. Paul's epistle was within reach of all his readers. If, on the other hand, St. Mark's Gospel was already in existence when St. Paul wrote his Epistle, we wonder why St. Paul should find it necessary to address his letter to the same gentile converts, as many commentators claim.

The Jews of Rome

The Epistle to the Romans has been described as the fullest and most profound of all St. Paul's letters : and the Romans, to whom the letter is addressed, have been described by St. Paul himself as "full of goodness and filled with all knowledge

---

[1] J. A. O'Flynn, *A Catholic Commentary on Holy Scripture*, 725c.

and capable of even advising one another" (15 : 14). Yet Paul is very anxious to pay them a personal visit, if the Romans will allow it. He hoped, perhaps, that by personal contact he could establish relations with the great body of his fellow-countrymen in Rome, and win them over for Christ. One of his first engagements three days after his arrival as a prisoner in Rome was with the leaders of the Jews there. He summoned them to confer with him and throughout a whole day they listened and argued (Acts 28 : 16).

There was much travelling to and fro at that time between Rome and the provinces. Roman Jews could exert an influence that might react favourably on Paul's work in the West, might even help to assuage the bitterness of his Jewish enemies nearer home in Judea. Jews led an exclusive, self-centred life. Members of the same family might be attending the Church and the Synagogue, and Paul's letter was likely to be read outside the Christian community. The tone of the letter is so conciliatory to the Jews, the forthright exposition of doctrine so characteristic of St. Paul is so cautiously tempered here, the letter in general is so preoccupied with the Mosaic Law and the Jewish question that the impression is left that this letter, for all its profundity of doctrine, was also intended to placate the Jews of Rome.

While Paul has no misgiving in connexion with his proposed visit to Spain, he is quite hesitant—almost apologetic—about the Roman visit, apologetic even for writing this letter. The explanation is that St. Paul was commissioned to preach the gospel to the gentiles. The Romans, to whom this letter is addressed, were outside the sphere of his commission. They were Jews, as is indicated by the internal evidence.

The Romans addressed not gentiles

After introducing himself to the Romans, St. Paul testifies that he has received the grace of the apostolate to preach submission to the faith throughout the gentile nations, *amongst whom you also are* (1 : 7). Rome was a gentile nation beyond all doubt. Why does St. Paul mention that his addressees are living amongst the gentiles? Does not this imply a distinction of nationality between the Romans and the gentiles? Further on he says: *I would not have you ignorant, brethren, that I have often planned to visit you . . . to reap some harvest amongst you also as amongst the gentiles that are left* (τοῖς λοιποῖς 1 : 13). He is referring to

Spain and the West, having finished his mission amongst the gentiles of the East. Note, however, that he does not say *amongst the other gentiles*, which would be the normal way of putting it, if the Romans also were gentiles.

He continues: *To the Greeks and Barbarians it is my duty* (ὀφειλέτης) *to preach the gospel. It is my personal desire* (τὸ κατ᾽ἐμὲ πρόθυμον) *to preach it to you also who are in Rome* (1 : 14). The Romans, therefore, were outside the sphere of Paul's missionary obligations. They were neither Greeks nor Barbarians. They were Jews; and it is personal urge, fundamentally no doubt spiritual, that has determined him to write this letter and pave the way for his proposed visit.

The strongest evidence of all is towards the end of the Epistle: *Rather daringly I have written to you, outside my commission, because of the grace given me by God to be a minister of Christ Jesus to the gentiles* (15 : 15). The meaning here is, as the order of words indicates, that St. Paul has taken a rather daring step in writing to the Romans, because they are outside the scope of his mission (ἀπὸ μέρους "outside the part assigned") which is to the gentiles. The phrase ἀπὸ μέρους explains τολμηροτέρως *rather boldly*, and is, in turn, explained by the following clause indicating the mission assigned him (Gal. 2 : 9). The usual version of this passage runs: "I have written to you *rather daringly in part*, because my mission is to the gentiles," that is, St. Paul is explaining why certain passages of his letter are written in a rather bold or daring strain. Others say that ἀπὸ μέρους does not refer to particular passages, but to the general authoritative tone of the letter—"rather daring to a certain degree." Some commentators actually pick out the daring passages (6 : 12–21 ; 8 : 9 ; 11 ; 17 ff.; 13 : 3 ff. ; 14 : 1–15) but analysis of these passages will reveal nothing daring. While ἀπὸ μέρους can undoubtedly bear the meaning *in part*, it cannot be so rendered here because in 15 : 24 where the context is exactly the same, the phrase is repeated and cannot possibly be rendered *in part*. The phrase ἀπὸ μέρους repeated in such immediate proximity in the same context, must be rendered in exactly the same way in each verse. Commentators, realizing the absurdity of rendering ἀπὸ μέρους *in part* in verse 24, have translated it *for a while*, a meaning which is nowhere found.

In 15 : 22–25 St. Paul says: *For which reason principally I was prevented from coming to see you* (i.e. preoccupation with his missionary work among the gentiles of the East), *but now having no place left in these quarters, and having a longing to come to you for many years past . . . on my way to Spain . . .for I count on seeing you on my way through . . . and on being escorted by you thither . . . if first I have full enjoyment of your company . . . outside my commission;* that is, his mission or commission is to the gentiles, not to Jews. Note the hesitant, faltering character of this passage. Commentators explain it by anacoluthon. It is rather hiatus, the speech of a man who is embarrassed, proposing to pay a visit, but not quite sure of his reception. He does not say: "On my way to Spain I will call in to see you." Nor: "I hope to be escorted thither when I have enjoyed your company," but tentatively, "if first I have enjoyed your company." There is nothing hesitant in his proposal to visit Spain. He was going there in his official capacity to preach to gentiles. The Romans were not gentiles. They were *outside his commission.* He had no official claim on their hospitality.

Commentators claim that St. Paul's reluctance to visit Rome is due to the fact that the Romans were not his spiritual children. He states in this context that it was a principle of his not to build on others' foundations (15 : 20), but this not by way of explaining his absence from Rome, rather to account for having finished his work in Eastern parts. He has omitted Asia Minor and Bithynia (Acts 16 : 6–7) and other countries already evangelized (cf. 1 Peter 1 : 1). He says it was his preoccupation with preaching the gospel in gentile countries which he mentions, that principally (τά πολλά) prevented him from visiting Rome. Another reason which is only hinted at, was his uncertainty of the reception he was likely to get from the Jews of Rome. Jews generally regarded Paul as a renegade.

Mildness towards the Jews

There are various other indications pointing to the conclusion that the Romans were Jewish converts. In the first chapter St. Paul, in proving the universality of sin, makes a scathing attack on the gentiles for their infidelity to God and their degenerate lives. It is a picture of unrelieved gloom and degradation, a terrible indictment, borne out indeed by the testimony of profane literature and history. But in dealing with the Jews in chapters II and III he takes a very different line.

In 3 : 9, identifying himself with his addressees, he says: *Have we an advantage then*? that is, have we Jews an advantage over the gentiles in our need for justification? Though his reply to this question is *not at all*, the instances he gives of Jewish sinfulness are all taken from the Old Testament, the psalms for the most part (Ps. 3 : 10–18), and therefore much less likely to offend the susceptibility of the Jews. Quotations from Scripture could be universal in their application. St. Paul's charges against the Jews are the essence of mildness compared with the charges brought by Christ: *Woe upon you Scribes and Pharisees, hypocrites that shut the door of heaven in men's faces. You will neither enter yourselves nor let others enter . . . that swallow up the property of widows . . . that make the proselyte twice as worthy of damnation as yourselves . . . blind fools . . . and have forgotten the weightier commandments of the law, justice, mercy and honour . . . whitened sepulchres . . . brood of vipers.* (Mt. 23 *passim*.)

St. Stephen said: *Stiffnecked race . . . you are forever resisting the Holy Spirit just as your fathers did . . . you also received the law dictated by angels and did not keep it* (Acts 7 : 51–53). We are told that on hearing this the Jews were cut to the heart and began to gnash their teeth at him (Acts 7 : 54). St. Paul is very careful to avoid giving any such offence to his audience. Speaking of the unconverted Jews generally he says: *For I bear witness for them that they have zeal for God, but not in accordance with right knowledge, for ignoring the justification which is from God, and seeking to establish their own, they have not submitted themselves to justification by God* (Romans 10 : 2–3). Could anything be milder or less offensive, considering the history of Jewish infidelity and treachery?

Again, while St. Paul mercilessly castigates the gentiles for their immoral lives he is quite apologetic when implying such a charge against his Roman friends. He is urging the Romans to a life of virtue in their new state: *For just as you made your members slaves to uncleanness and lawlessness, even so now make your members enslaved to justice and holiness* (6 : 19). But before making this statement he cautiously qualifies it with the preface: *What I am going to say is characteristic of human nature* (ἀνθρώπινον) *because of the weakness of the flesh.* St. Paul would never think it necessary to make such an apology if he were dealing with gentile converts. Here he is sparing the feelings of those still adhering to the Law.

There are three chapters devoted to the Jewish question, that is, proving that God was not unjust in excluding the Jews from his Kingdom on earth. Would not gentiles accept the position without any proof? The Pharaoh of the Exodus is introduced as instancing God's omnipotence and his hardening of the hearts of those who flout his will. Pharaoh's case was illustrative of God's omnipotence, but it was also an exact parallel of the Jews' own case. But St. Paul does not point the moral—Pharaoh was destroyed for persistently opposing God's will. St. Paul knew of such Jews, *vessels of wrath* like Pharaoh whose cup of iniquity had been filled. But he refers to them only obliquely, hypothetically, and commentators here again fall back on the anacoluthon for explanation. But there is in reality no missing link: *But if God, though wishing to manifest his wrath and make known his power, has endured in much patience vessels of wrath fitted for destruction, [he has endured it] in order to show forth the wealth of his glory to vessels of pity* (9 : 22–23). The "if" sentence has categorical force and is equivalent to *God has endured*. . . . This is an instance of Paul's mildness when addressing Jews directly. When speaking to the Thessalonians he said: *the Jews, the men who killed the Lord Jesus and the prophets and persecuted us; the men who displease God and show themselves the enemies of mankind . . . they must always be filling up the measure of their sins, and now it is God's final vengeance that has fallen on them* (2 Thess. 2 : 1). The Thessalonians were not Jews and St. Paul had no inhibition when talking to them about Jews. His forthrightness was always tempered with prudence and tactfulness.

Under the Law

St. Paul definitely implies that the Romans whom he is addressing had lived under the Law, that is, under the abrogated Law of Moses: *For you are not now under the Law but under grace* (6 : 14). Gentiles never lived under the Law. Again he appeals to his addressees as people who know the law (7 : 1). The Mosaic Law is in question and gentiles can hardly be expected to know it. Individual gentiles might have some knowledge of the Law. St. Paul takes it that the body of Christians he is addressing had knowledge of the Law. The Jews studied the Law even in their primary schools, and read it regularly in the synagogues. It is far more reasonable to interpret *people who know the law* as Jews.

Further on St. Paul says: *So that you, my brethren, have died to the Law through the body of Christ* (7 : 4). Gentiles who were never under the Law and under no obligation to submit to the Law, could not be said in any sense to have died to the Law.

There is the much discussed passage 7 : 7–25. What bearing has this on the question whether Paul's addressees were Jews or gentiles? Paul again identifies himself with his hearers: *When we were in the power of the flesh the sinful passions aroused by the law worked through our members producing a harvest for death. But as it is, we have been released from the law, having died to that wherein we were held captive, so that in our new life we are slaves of the spirit, not slaves of the letter as of old* (7 : 5–6). Here surely the Apostle is speaking about converts from the Mosaic Law, not about gentiles.

The Mosaic Law was abrogated by the death of Christ. *Christ was the end of the Law unto justification for everyone who believes in him.* (Ros. 10 : 4.) After Christ's death the Law ceased to have any validity as a Law. It was still on the statute book so to speak, but like any other piece of repealed legislation nothing now remained but the letter of the law. At the Council of Jerusalem (49 A.D.) the Mosaic Law was formally set aside. The vast majority of the Jewish people, however, refused to accept Christ and persisted in adhering to the Law as a sufficient means of salvation; and "Judaizing" Christians, as they were called, tried to impose the Law on Christian converts, insisting that circumcision was still essential for salvation, equally with baptism.

It was this teaching that drew from St. Paul the grave admonition to the Galatians, *Lo I Paul tell you that if you become circumcised Christ will be of no avail for you. Again I bear testimony to every man who is circumcised, that he is bound to carry out the Law in its entirety. In claiming to get justification through the Law you have been cut adrift from Christ, you have fallen away from grace.* (Gal. 5 : 2–4.) This passage clearly means that once the Mosaic Law was abrogated, those who still adhered to it or embraced it were bound by all its obligations (*the Law in its entirety*), but could not perform a single precept of the Law because they were cut adrift from Christ and grace. This had been the position of Paul himself before his conversion. It had been also the position of Jewish Roman Christians before their conversion. It was still the position of the vast body of Jews in

Rome and elsewhere, who placed their hope of salvation in the Law.

The meaning of chapter VII

The doctrine of *Romans* 7 : 7–25 is exactly the same as the doctrine of *Galatians* 5 : 2–4, namely the utter futility of the abrogated Mosaic Law as a means of salvation. Commentators are mistaken, as we hope to show later in detail, in interpreting this passage of *Romans* as giving a true picture of the spiritual life of Israel under the regime of the Law—that its purpose is to show the impotence of the Law during its regime, against the forces of concupiscence; that the Law deserved to be set aside as having provoked the divine anger in multiplying transgressions.

St. Paul is speaking here of the Law as it stood in his own time, that is abrogated, repealed, set aside by the death of Christ, and formally by the Council of Jerusalem. He told the Galatians plainly and bluntly that the man who sought justification through the Law, was cut adrift from Christ and had fallen from grace. He is teaching the same doctrine to the Romans—to the Roman Christians directly, but principally to the great body of Roman Jews who profess to work out their salvation by observance of the Law. To the Romans St. Paul conveys his teaching in a subtle, somewhat enigmatic manner, by giving a concrete case of a man who while living *outside the Law*, that is under the Natural Law, had enjoyed God's grace and friendship (ἔζων *I lived* 7 : 9), but who, on embracing the abrogated Mosaic Law, fell into grave sin (ἀπέθανον 7 : 10) through disobeying a precept of the Law; and despite his most earnest efforts, failed to recover God's grace; not only that, but failed to perform a single salutary action, and became the helpless slave of sin.

The reason of this man's helpless plight is that, under the abrogated Law, he is cut away from Christ the source of grace; and without grace, his actions are on a purely natural level and will not be accepted by God as fulfilling any divine obligation. The Speaker or Objector who is introduced in *Romans* 7 : 7 was able to perform his obligations towards God under the Natural Law, *outside the Law* (V. 9), because he was united through faith with the promised Redeemer. On the other hand, the abrogated Law which he embraced in good faith is now completely divorced from Christ. It has entered in on the side of sin against Christ (Ros. 5 : 20). The man, therefore, who has put his trust for salvation in this abrogated Law is incapable, for want of grace, of performing any of the precepts of the Law, though bound by all of them, Christ being the sole source of grace.

St. Paul warning the Galatians against Judaizers, who tried to impose on them the abrogated Law as necessary for salvation, spoke out plainly telling them of the consequences. There does not appear to have been any Judaizing problem in the Roman community which St. Paul is addressing. These Christians had a thorough knowledge of the Gospel, and were famed for their loyalty to its teaching. The teaching in 7 : 7–25, conveyed through the rhetorical figure the Diatribe, is intended for the Jews in the background who still adhered to the Law. If St. Paul spoke directly and bluntly as he had spoken to the Galatians who were mostly Gentiles, telling the Roman Jews that the Law on which they now staked their salvation was a *law of sin and death* (Ros. 8 : 2) they would have gnashed their teeth in anger against him, as they had done to St. Stephen. His method in this delicate situation is indirect and figurative but none the less comprehensive from the viewpoint of doctrine. The Jew, that is the unregenerate Jew who is *depending on the flesh* (Ros. 7 : 5), depending on the resources of unaided human nature, completely divorced from grace—this being the condition of those living under the abrogated Law—is described as a violator even of the Natural Law, and will be judged by the gentile who has no written law but obeys the voice of conscience (Ros. 2 : 26–27). When the Speaker cries out in desperation *who will deliver me from this body of death?* the reply is, *God through Christ Jesus* (7 : 24). Under the New Dispensation salvation for Jew and gentile is through faith in Christ.

Speaking of the Galatians, who were admittedly gentiles in the majority, St. Paul reminds them that formerly they had no knowledge of the true God. *You were the slaves of gods who had no divine nature* (Gal. 4 : 8). The Romans, in their pre-Christian days, *were the slaves of sin* (Ros. 6 : 20). There is no suggestion that they worshipped false Gods. A thorough knowledge of the Scriptures on their part is implied. Even their unregenerate brethren *are jealous for God's honour* (10 : 2). Christian gentiles throughout the world are reminded of their obligation to the Jewish nation. They are only the fruit of the wild olive *grafted on to the true olive's stock* (Ros. 11 : 24). *I am speaking now to you gentiles* (11 : 13) says St. Paul reminding gentiles everywhere of their duty to the Jews. Hitherto he has been addressing Jews. Indeed, he says, it is the duty of the gentiles everywhere, who have been privileged to share the spiritual gifts of the Jews, to contribute in turn to their temporal needs (Ros. 15 : 27). In fact, as far as is possible as Apostle of the gentiles, Paul himself will make the most of his ministry in the hope of stirring up to emulation his own flesh and blood and saving some of them (Ros. 11 : 13). The plight of the Jews is a source of great sorrow for him and continuous heartfelt anguish. For the sake of his brethren, his own kinsmen by race, he is ready to make any sacrifice, even to be annihilated from the presence of Christ (9 : 2–3), whose love transcends for St. Paul all human consideration (Ros. 8 : 35). This attitude of conciliation and concern for Jews would scarcely be pertinent in a letter addressed to a community with a majority of gentiles.

The meaning of chapter XIV

It is maintained that Chapter XIV supplies evidence for the predominantly gentile character of the community which St. Paul is addressing in the Epistle to the Romans. He is appealing to the strong to have respect for the scruples of their weaker brethren in the matter of meats and observance of certain holy days. The *strong* are interpreted as gentile converts and the *weak* as Jewish converts. The inference rather to be drawn from this Chapter is that St. Paul is addressing an exclusively Jewish body. *I know and I am convinced that there is nothing unclean in itself. It is only when a man believes a thing to be unclean that it becomes unclean for him* (Ros. 14 : 14). Would St. Paul have been likely to ask gentile converts to abstain from meats which they had been using all their lives and which they were entitled to use on every count, in order to humour the unfounded scruples of a Jewish minority? Could he reasonably expect compliance with that request? Is it not much more probable that the strong were those, who, like St. Paul himself, were now convinced that taboos in the matter of food were abolished in the Christian regime; but accustomed as they had been to abstain, would be likely to do so now also for the edification of their weaker brethren ? That would be a reasonable request. The weak in *Galatians* who were endeavouring to honour the precepts of the Mosaic Law get short shrift from St. Paul, and the question has been asked, why this marked difference in his attitude to the weak in *Romans*?

The Roman Christians in question were well instructed in their faith *full of good will . . . knowing all you need know, so that you can give advice to one another if need be* (15 : 14). There is no question of doctrine involved in the differences that arose in the Roman community. St. Paul is appealing to individuals for the self-sacrifice that makes for domestic unity and charity. The Galatian scene was different. There, a small section of the community were trying to impose the Mosaic Law on the whole community, the small section being of Jewish nationality, or at all events, Judaizers. There is no suggestion of parties in the Roman community. The *weak* and the *strong* mentioned are not listed on a numerical basis. The weak are the scrupulous whose conscience forbade them certain liberties denied by the Mosaic Law. The strong are those who, like St. Paul himself, are convinced that there is no longer any uncleanness in the matter of food, and no obligation whatever to recognise the customs of the Law in this or other matters. Parties are not formed on such lines of cleavage.

Taking it, as some commentators do, that the weak are Jewish Christians and the strong gentile Christians, one wonders would Jewish Christians be disedified at seeing gentiles using the meats in question. Is it not more likely that their quarrels are with fellow-Jews from whom they hoped to expect better? St. Paul admits that there is no food unclean for Christians, but appeals to the strong-minded, whose convictions in this matter are like his own, to respect the scruples of the weaker brethren, who might otherwise be influenced by the example around them to do violence to their conscience. For the sake of food, he advises them, *do not disturb a brother's peace of mind* (Ros. 14 : 14). He appeals to all of them to refrain from judging their neighbour's action and to avoid discussions and criticisms that will spoil their domestic peace.

There is no similarity between the situation in Rome and that of Galatia. It is only in the last chapters of *Romans* that any reference is made to domestic differences. These are the petty quarrels that might ruffle the surface of any family life. They certainly were not of such a nature as to call for the writing of St. Paul's epistle, as is suggested. If so, why does he leave all reference to these differences to the last and refer to them only when he is taking leave of his correspondents? The omission of any reference whatever to circumcision in the domestic differences of the Romans, would indicate that they were all converts from Judaism and all circumcised. If this was a mixed community of Jews and gentiles, like the Galatian community, it is hardly conceivable that among the disputes concerning the observance of the Mosaic Law, the question of circumcision would not have emerged in some form. But there is not a word about circumcision. The domestic troubles in this Roman community had to do principally with meats. The suave-spoken trouble makers, who feigned an interest in the welfare of the community, were concerned for their own stomachs according to St. Paul[1] (Ros. 16 : 18). They were not willing to forego anything in the nature of food. It was not a quarrel about principle such as characterised mixed communities of Jew and gentile Christians.

By what right dost thou bind gentiles . . . ?

If the Roman community which St. Paul is addressing had been, as commentators maintain, a mixed community of Jews and gentile Christians—with gentiles in the majority—by what authority could St. Paul have admonished the gentiles to conform to Jewish standards in the matter of food? Was not this the very thing for which he had rebuked St. Peter in Antioch? St. Peter, we are told, had been eating with the gentiles until certain delegates arrived from Jerusalem. These brought such pressure on Peter that he and even Barnabas, who had helped Paul to found the Church of Antioch, began to draw back and hold themselves aloof. St. Paul tells us he opposed Cephas openly and *he stood self condemned . . . I said to Cephas in front of them all . . . by what right dost thou bind the gentiles to live like Jews?* (Gal. 2 : 12–14). Surely Paul would not himself have advocated the very course of conduct in Rome for which he rebuked Peter publicly in Antioch. The evidence of chapter XIV points to the strong probability that the Roman community was exclusively Jewish in nationality. Their differences were of a domestic nature. St. Paul advises the

---

[1]It would appear that "the strong" in this Roman community were quoting St. Paul's teaching to the Galatians against their opponents. This would explain *the edifying and pious language* (16 : 18), and explain also Paul's personal concern for the situation in Rome.

strong-minded to make a sacrifice for the edification of the less strong-minded in the interest of unity. This was his own custom. *With the scrupulous I behaved myself like one who is scrupulous, to win the scrupulous.* (1 Cor. 9 : 22.)

St. Paul's Epistle to the Romans is not a treatise on Christianity. There are far too many omissions to justify such a description. The work, however, might be fairly described as an Introduction to Christianity written especially for Jews. The Jews professed to believe that the Mosaic Law was of itself sufficient for salvation; and that by virtue of the Law heirship to the promises made to Abraham and the patriarchs, heirship to the kingdom which the Messias would establish, was theirs exclusively. They rejected Christ as the promised Messias. In this letter addressed to the Roman Christians St. Paul emphasises the primacy of Christ in the economy of salvation to the complete exclusion of the Mosaic Law which was hitherto binding on the Jews. The faith of the Roman Christians whom he is addressing, is favourably spoken of throughout the whole world (Ros. 1 : 8). They were excellently instructed and remain true to the pattern of instruction in which they were moulded (6 : 17). *They are full of goodness, replete with all knowledge and able even to counsel one another* in matters of discipline (15 : 14). *You are renowned all over the world for your loyalty to the gospel, and I am proud of you* (16 : 19).

St. Paul's eagerness to visit Rome

Why in these circumstances did St. Paul think it necessary to address them in this the most elaborate of his epistles? If these Roman Christians were gentiles for the most part like the Galatians, and if Paul feared the influence of Judaizers in their midst, surely the Epistle to the Galatians, which was now some ten years in circulation, would have been sufficient to counter that danger. And even if Paul experienced an apostolic urge to write this famous letter to the Roman Christians, who were not his spiritual children, why was he so eager to make personal contact with the Romans? Why was he so hesitant and punctilious in his approach, so careful to emphasise that he had no official claim on their hospitality? Surely he had nothing to fear in the way of rebuke or discourtesy from these excellent Christians who were so loyal to the teaching of the gospel. He did fear the Jews of Judea and asked for the prayers of the Roman community in this connexion (16 : 31). He says that his purpose in visiting the Roman Christians is to share a spiritual gift with them for their mutual encouragement (Ros. 1 : 11) and to make holiday with them (16 : 32). St. Paul, it would seem, was anxious to make contact with the great body of unregenerate Jews in Rome, whose salvation he had deeply at heart, and he hoped through this letter to conciliate their attitude towards him. They would be likely to read this letter or hear of its contents from their friends. Paul was suspect in the eyes of Jews, and had reason to fear them. He had collided with the Jews of Corinth. Hitherto he had not clashed with the great body of Roman Jews, and here perhaps was a field in which he could labour with hopes of return (1 : 13).

It is certainly significant that almost immediately on his arrival at Rome as a prisoner, Paul's first recorded action was to summon the leaders of the Jews to an interview. He is careful to explain to them that his appeal to Caesar did not imply that he had any fault to find with his own nation. *I am one who has done nothing to the prejudice of our people or of our ancestral customs* (Ac. 28 : 17). We are told that *he bore his testimony and told them about the Kingdom of God, trying to convince them from Moses and the prophets concerning Jesus, from dawn till dusk* (Ac. 28 : 23). The theme of *Romans* is *justification by God through faith in Christ, a justification to which the Law and the Prophets bore testimony.* (Ros. 3 : 21). This also was the theme of his discussion with the Jews of Rome *from dawn till dusk, trying to convince them from Moses and the Prophets concerning Jesus.* . . . The liberal quotation from the Old Testament throughout the epistle suggests that St. Paul was writing for an audience that had a thorough knowledge of the Scriptures. Christ is the Saviour promised in the *Law and the Prophets. All the words that have been written have been written for our instruction.* (Ros. 15 : 4). The New Dispensation of Christ and grace is the logical outcome of the Old.

One feels that in the Epistle to the Romans St. Paul had such an interview in mind, though it occurred in circumstances other than he had anticipated. There is a general tone of sweet reasonableness and good fellowship towards the Jews, but no compromise on doctrine.

It was only after this interview that Paul realised the hopelessness of preaching Christ to the Jews at this juncture. St. Luke sums up the result: Some were convinced by his words, others refused to believe. They departed at variance with one another, Paul having spoken *one word* to them: *Well did the Holy Spirit put it, speaking through the mouth of Isaias the prophet to your fathers. "Go to this people and tell them; listening you will listen, but never understand. Looking you will look but never see. For the heart of this people has become gross and their ears have become dull from listening and their eyes have been strained from looking, lest they should ever hear with their ears and understand with their heart and turn to me that I may heal them"* (Ac. 28 : 17ff).

With this *one word* Paul took leave of the Jews, a wiser and sadder man.

Chapter Three

JUSTIFICATION THROUGH FAITH IN CHRIST

IN the opening chapter of the *Epistle to the Romans* St. Paul presents his credentials. He is the slave of Jesus Christ, an apostle by virtue of a special call, marked off for the preaching of the gospel,—the *good news which God had announced beforehand in the sacred writings concerning his own Son* (Ros. 1 : 3).

The first instalment of the record of good news occurs in Genesis (3 : 15). Adam, the head of the human race, lost for himself and mankind, with a single exception, the supernatural privileges with which God had endowed him, the *glory of God*, as St. Paul expresses it. Then God promised a Redeemer. The *seed of the woman* would crush the serpent's head. In the course of time the promise became more definite. Abraham received a special call from God and a promise that through him and his seed all the nations of the earth shall be blessed (Gen. 12 : 3). The promise is renewed to Isaac, Abraham's son (Gen. 26 : 4), and to Jacob, one of Isaac's sons (Gen. 28 : 4).

At a later period the idea of a personal Redeemer emerges more definitely. Ultimately the royal house of David is appointed for the special honour (2 Kgs. 7:14). Bethlehem, the city of David, is to be the Saviour's birthplace (Mic. 5 : 2). He will be born of a virgin (Is. 7 : 14). The character of his reign was outlined. His rule was to be guided by justice and his dominion to be universal (Ps. 2 : 8 ; 71 : 2–4). His humiliations, sufferings and violent death were also prophesied with wealth of detail (Ps. 21; Is. 53).

There is one truth that is continually emphasised in the Old Testament prophecies, namely that victory over sin and guilt can be realised only by the intervention of a Mediator whom God in his mercy has willed to send.

St. Paul's mission is to preach the gospel, of which he says with characteristically Greek understatement, that *he is not ashamed*, for in the gospel is *a power from God for salvation for everyone who believes, Jew and Greek; for therein is revealed justification by God through faith* (Ros. 1 : 16–17),—faith in Christ, as we shall see.

The subject of the gospel is Jesus Christ, true man as shown by his descent from the house of David; true God as shown by his resurrection from the dead—*in holiness of spirit proved to be the Son of God by his miraculous power on the occasion of his resurrection from the dead* (Ros. 1 : 4). Holiness is the special attribute of God. That Christ had the divine attribute of holiness is proved because only God, the author of life, could lay down his life and take it up at will.

Christ the promised Redeemer

Is Christ, whose life and preaching the gospel records, the Redeemer promised to Adam and through Adam to all mankind? Is Christ the *seed of the woman* who was destined to crush the serpent's head? St. Paul says this has been clearly revealed in the gospel. The gospel *reveals the mystery hidden from mankind through countless ages* (Ros. 16 : 26). The Law and the Prophets— the Old Testament—bore testimony beforehand to the Saviour who was to come. But prophecy is of its nature obscure, and its full significance is seen only in the light of the event prophesied.

The Messias, the promised Redeemer of mankind, would belong to the house of David and would possess the fulness of God's holy spirit (Is. 11 : 1–2). *Then shall the eyes of the blind be opened and the ears of the deaf shall be unstopped, then shall the lame leap like a deer* prophesies Isaias (35 : 5). When the Baptist from his prison sent messengers to ask Christ *art thou he who is to come or are we to expect another?* his reply was: *Go tell John that the blind see, the lame walk* . . . (Mt. 11, 4). On witnessing the teachings and miracles of Christ the Jews asked themselves whether he was the promised Redeemer (Lk. 7 : 16 ; Jn. 6 : 14). On occasions Jesus admitted that the prophecies were fulfilled in him. *You search the Scriptures; they give testimony of me* he replied to the Scribes and Pharisees when they upbraided him for healing on the Sabbath. And again, *if you believe Moses you would believe in me, for he wrote of me* (Jn. 5 : 39). He reminded the Apostles also of the prophecies describing his passion, death and resurrection: *Now we go up to Jerusalem and all will be accomplished that was written by the prophets about the Son of Man . . .* (Lk. 18 : 31–33). Speaking to the disciples from Emmaus the risen Christ said *how slow and dull of heart you are in believing all that the prophets have said. Was not the Messias obliged to suffer, and so enter into his glory? Then he began with Moses and in each prophet through all the Scriptures he explained to them the prophecies about himself* (Lk. 24 : 25–27). A special feature of the gospel of St. Matthew is showing how prophecies concerning the coming Redeemer have been fulfilled in Christ.

Christ, then, is the Redeemer promised to Adam and through Adam to mankind. He is the Son of God equal to the Father in all things. At his baptism in the Jordan and Transfiguration the truth was proclaimed from heaven : *Thou art my beloved Son; in whom I am well pleased* (Mk. 1 : 11). *This is my beloved Son; hear ye him* (Mk. 9 : 7). At his trial when challenged by the High Priest, *art thou the Christ the Son of the blessed God? Jesus said to him* [*Yes*], *thou hast said it* (Mk. 14 : 61). By assuming human nature, Christ was able to substitute himself voluntarily for all his brethren, and make himself the surety for their sins. *God laid on him the iniquity of us all* (Is. 53 : 6). As God his every act was of infinite value. He was able to make full atonement to God for the outrage offered by sin to the divine majesty. *When Christ died on the cross God*, says St. Paul, *was in Christ, reconciling the world to himself* (2 Cor. 5 : 19). *Christ washed us from our sins in his own blood* (Apoc. 1 : 5). The gospel reveals that Christ is the sole Redeemer, the one and only Mediator between God and man. *No one comes to the Father except through me* (Jn. 14 : 15). *In no other is there salvation* (Ac. 4–12).

The New Dispensation

The gospel also reveals the manner in which God is to be worshipped henceforth. It is a *power for salvation*. The Old Dispensation has been set aside, fulfilled in Christ. The distinction between Jew and Gentile has been erased. A new and everlasting covenant has been instituted, ratified by the blood of Christ. The gospel, furthermore, reveals that Christ, in order to continue his work of salvation, handed over to an organisation of men the power entrusted to himself by God. *As the Father hath sent me so I also send you* (Jn. 20 : 20). Membership of this organisation, which is conferred by the sacrament of baptism, is necessary for salvation. *He who believes and is baptised shall be saved* (Mk. 16 : 16).

Before St. Paul proceeds to deal directly with the question of justification, there is a long digression showing the need for justification as illustrated by the sinful state of mankind, Jew and Gentile. In chapter iii, he resumes his thesis: *But now without reference to the Law, justification has been made manifest, attested by the Law and the prophets, justification by God through faith in Christ, for all who believe in him* (Ros. 3 : 21–22).

The Greek δικαιοσύνη θεοῦ is here usually translated *the justice or justness of God*. It is argued that in classical Greek the word δικαιοσύνη has nowhere the meaning *justification*. But the justice of God, if the term is taken in its ordinary signification, is much more clearly illustrated in the Old Testament than in the Gospel. There can be no doubt whatever that the verb δικαιόω is used in the Septuagint and in the New Testament with the meaning *to justify, to make just*, as τυφλόω means *to make blind*, or ἐλευθερόω *to make free*. St. Paul uses δικαιόω in this sense, θεὸς ὁ δικαιῶν *God it is who makes men just* (Ros. 8 : 33), not merely *declares just*, as some of the Reformers held.

A judge, through ignorance of the truth, may pronounce a man just who is not just, but God the author of truth, cannot do so. The substantive δικαιοσύνη here, and in similar contexts, has a connotation corresponding to the verb. It is a verbal noun, and means *justification, the making just*. The Greek of St. Paul's day was a living language and adaptable to the expression of new ideas. Surely it will not be contended that there is no word in the Greek language for the Christian concept of justification. The context here clearly shows that the concept in question is *making the sinner just*, that is removing his guilt. That the substantive δικαιοσύνη has the significance of the verb, is indicated by the clause describing the means or manner of the *action*, justification *through* faith in Christ: and can be adequately expressed by the form *God justifies through faith in Christ*. There are, of course, other significations of δικαιοσύνη as we shall see presently. The version *a justice* or *"justness" of God* does not give the sense of the Greek. St. Paul is concerned here not with the justice of God, but with the justice of the sinner which God effects through the sinner's faith in Christ. The metaphysical question of the relation between divine justice and the justice of the sinner does not arise.

Theme of the Epistle

The main theme of the Epistle to the Romans is *justification by God through faith in Christ*, and the implications of this justification in the spiritual life of mankind. Expressed in simpler terms, the subject of the epistle is: salvation for all mankind without exception is secured by faith in Christ the Redeemer, not by the works prescribed by the Mosaic Law. *For by the works of the Law no flesh shall be justified in his sight. For through the Law comes knowledge of sin* (3 : 20). St. Paul, it must be remembered, is here speaking of the Mosaic Law which was abrogated by the death of Christ and formally set aside by the Council of Jerusalem (A.D. 49). The Law during the period of its regime, we may state in passing, was on a completely different footing.

Justification means the remission of sin and the restoration of the sinner to God's grace and friendship. That this operation by God in the soul of the sinner is effected through faith in the Redeemer promised by God after Adam's sin, has been true for all time and will remain true to the end. After the sin of our first parents in Paradise, God cursed the tempter who had deceived them into disobeying God's command. He also placed enmity between *the seed of the woman* and *the seed of the serpent*, and in the struggle promised victory to *the seed of the woman*. The hostile forces were set in antagonism for all time. The issue was knit. On one side *the seed of the woman*, the promised Redeemer, to whom victory was assured; on the other side *the seed of the serpent*, —Satan and the powers of darkness. All mankind have to take one side or the other in the combat. There can be no neutrality. Christ's statement, *he who is not with me is against me* (Mt. 12 : 30), was true from the beginning. Man's sole hope of victory is union with the promised Redeemer. Faith in God implies faith in the Redeemer, because God cannot prove faithless to his promise.

The Mosaic Law

Some thirteen hundred years before the coming of Christ God entered into a covenant with his chosen people, the Israelites, by which they freely undertook to perform the obligations imposed on them by the Mosaic Law in return for great privileges. These obligations of the Law bound the Israelites under severe sanctions. The Law was to retain its validity *until the coming of the seed of the woman* (Gal. 3 : 19). The Law, while obligatory on the Israelites and on the Israelites alone, was at no time capable of itself of winning justification or salvation (Ros. 8 : 3). Its purpose was to prepare mankind for the coming of the promised Redeemer, and all its efficacy derived from faith in the Redeemer. The Redeemer would bring the Law to its fulfilment and usher in a new era, the New Dispensation.

The gospel reveals that the new era has begun (νυνί Ros. 3 : 21); that the Law had been abrogated, set aside fulfilled (χώρις νόμου); that Christ is the promised Redeemer, *the seed of the woman;* that justification or remission of sin is possible only for those who believe in Christ and acknowledge his divinity. Union with the promised Redeemer has been at all periods of mankind's history the one way of salvation. The great majority of the Jews refused to accept Christ or acknowledge his divinity. They professed to work out their salvation by obeying the precepts of the Mosaic Law, which no longer had any validity. *Ignoring the justification that comes from God and seeking to establish a justification of their own, they refused to submit to the justification by God* (Ros. 10 : 3). The one and only justification by God, according to St. Paul, is through faith in the divinity of Christ.

In a later section we shall deal with the question of the abrogation of the Law. We have seen, in bare outline, that the gospel reveals Christ, the Son of God as the Messias, the promised Redeemer. The gospel also makes it manifest that faith in the divinity of Christ is essential for justification.

Faith in the divinity of Christ

St. John tells us that it is faith in Jesus that makes us children of God; that is, by faith in Jesus man recovers the status lost by Adam's sin (1 : 2). Justification restores the sinner to that level. St. Paul speaks of the *man who belongs to Jesus by faith* (Ros. 3 : 26). Faith hands over the sinner to Christ, entitling him to a share in Christ's patrimony,—*coheirs with Christ.* (Ros. 8 : 17).

During Christ's public life, faith in the recipient of his miraculous favours is the first essential required. When the blind men were following him crying out *have mercy on us, O Son of David,* Jesus asks them, *do you believe that I can do this for you?*

And on hearing them profess their faith, he touched their eyes saying, *according to your faith be it done unto you.* And their eyes were opened (Mt. 9 : 27–30).

When the chief of the Synagogue asks Christ to save his daughter, his reply is, *believe only and she shall be safe* (Lk. 8 : 50). The cures of the paralytic man, of the woman who had suffered from an infirmity for twelve years, Jesus ascribed to their faith (Mk. 5 : 25 ff.). The expression *thy faith hath saved thee* very frequently occurs in the gospel narrative. Before raising Lazarus to life, Christ publicly claimed the authority of the Father for the miracle he was about to perform and put Martha's faith to the test, *I am the Resurrection and the Life: believest thou this?* (Jn. 11 : 27). Faith is the indispensable condition of his miracles. The gospel tells us that at Nazareth he wrought not many miracles because they did not believe in him (Mt. 13 : 58).

The faith of the pagan centurion at Capharnaum, who asked Jesus to heal his sick servant, has been enshrined in the liturgy of the Church. *Verily I say to you I have not found so great faith in Israel. And I say to you that many gentiles shall come and shall sit down at the feast of eternal life in the Kingdom of Heaven, while the children of Israel, who were the first to be called to the banquet, shall be cast out on account of their unbelief* (Mt. 8 : 12).

On one occasion, when Christ was probing deep for faith, he seemed not even to spare the feelings of his subject. In the region of Tyre and Sidon the woman of Canaan was following Christ and his disciples importuning him to cure her daughter who was *grievously troubled with a devil.... Send her away*, said the disciples. Christ said his mission was only to the people of Israel,—the gentiles being reserved for his disciples. But she persisted in imploring him, *Lord help me.* Then he said, *it is not good to take the bread of the children and cast it to the dogs. Yea, Lord*, said she, *but the whelps also eat of the crumbs that fall from the tables of their masters.* Christ, magnanimously atoning for his seeming callousness, reverently addresses her, *Lady*—as he had addressed his Mother on an occasion when she, too, refused to be denied her request—*great is thy faith. Be it done to thee as thou dost will* (Mt. 15 : 22–28).

To Magdalene, when she cast herself at his feet and washed them with her tears, he said, *thy sins are forgiven thee ... thy faith hath saved thee. Go in peace* (Lk. 7 : 5). At Calvary when his enemies were hurling mockeries at him, *let him come down from the cross and we will believe in him*, the thief who was hanging on the gibbet beside him said, *Lord, remember me when thou comest into thy Kingdom* (Lk. 23 : 42). The immediate and generous response shows the welcome Christ had for this act of faith in his divinity at the moment when, in the throes of an ignominious death, he was to all appearance defeated and discredited.

Before ascending into heaven, when Christ sent his Apostles to continue his mission throughout the world, again it is faith he insists upon: *He that believeth and is baptised shall be saved; he that believeth not shall be condemned* (Mt. 16 : 16). God, says St. John, sent his Son into the world not to judge the world, but that the world may be saved by him. *He that believes in him is not judged. But he that does not believe is already judged, because he believes not in the name of the only begotten Son of God* (Jn. 3 : 16–18).

"Faith in the divinity of Jesus", says Dom Columba Marmion, "is according to the designs of the Father the first thing needful in order to share in the divine life; faith in the divinity of Jesus Christ bears with it all the revealed truths. All revelation, it may be said, is contained in this supreme testimony God gives us that Jesus Christ is his Son, and all faith is likewise contained in the acceptation of this testimony."[1]

The Romans to whom St. Paul wrote the Epistle were well versed in Christian doctrine. They were held in high esteem in the Christian world of the day: *I know that you are full of good will, knowing all you need to know, so that you can give advice to one another if need be* (Ros. 15 : 14). St. Paul writes to them only *by way of refreshing their memory*. The point he wants particularly to emphasise is that from Christ and Christ only come all the graces of forgiveness and salvation, all spiritual riches—*life in Christ*—all the supernatural fruitfulness with which the world of souls abounds.

There was a large colony of Jews, estimated at about fifty thousand, in Rome at this time, the vast majority of whom still adhered to the Mosaic Law, and placed all their hope of salvation in the *works of the Law*. St. Paul, as we have already suggested, is concerned for the salvation of his countrymen, and hopes through the Christian body to reach the souls of these, the vast

[1]*Christ the Life of the Soul*, p. 130.

majority, who still cling to Judaism. The one point of doctrine which he stresses in the Epistle, is that Christ, whom the Jews reject, is the one and only Redeemer, the one and only Mediator between God and mankind, and that only by union with Christ, through faith, can sin be forgiven and salvation secured.

Justification

Justification is essential for all men, *for all have sinned and have forfeited the glory of God, being justified as a free gift through his love, by means of the Redemption which is in Christ Jesus* (Ros. 3 : 23–24). All have sinned in Adam's sin (Ros. 5 : 12), even those who have never been conscious of any deliberate sin; and all have lost the divine privileges—*the glory of God*—the grace and justice to which they were entitled as children and heirs of God. All became slaves of Satan and are born children of wrath (Eph. 2 : 3). Therefore all need forgiveness.

Justification restores the sinner to the supernatural status lost by Adam's sin. It is a free gift of God. Neither a man's faith, which is also a free gift, nor anything man himself is capable of doing, can merit as something due, the privilege of justification. The Jews professed faith in God and claimed that by *doing the works of the Law* they were entitled to justification. St. Paul emphasises that justification comes solely from God's love or grace, as a result of the ransom or redemption which Christ paid in his own person by his sufferings and death on the cross. Under the Old Dispensation the works of the Law were obligatory for the Israelites, but the spiritual efficacy of these works depended on faith in Christ. The Law was a *pedagogue leading to Christ* (Gal. 3 : 24), and divorced from Christ ceases to have any significance, as St. Paul illustrates in *Romans* vii. In every period in the history of mankind *men are freely justified by God's grace through the Redemption there is in Christ Jesus* (Ros. 3 : 24).

St. Paul proceeds to illustrate this truth in a remarkably vivid manner. In every age of the world when God forgives sin, it is by the authority of the dead Christ on the *cross whom God set before himself* (προέθετο)—*a victim of atonement through faith by virtue of the shedding of his own blood—as proof of God's justice in forgiving, in his forbearance, sins committed before Christ* (προγεγονότων); *to be the proof of his justice [in forgiving sins] at the present time* (Ros. 3 : 25–26).

St. Paul here argues as if God's justice in forgiving the sins of men were challenged. Was God just in forgiving sins through his forbearance (ἀνοχῇ) or mercy? If, for instance, God was just in failing to forgive the sins of the angels, how can he be just in forgiving men? How is he just in forgiving sins committed before the Redemption actually took place, before Christ actually paid the ransom—the sin of David for instance? Is forgiveness of sin not altogether a matter of forbearance or mercy on God's part? How is God's justice involved, seeing that justification is a free gift from God? What right or title in this connexion has the sinner which the angels had not?

God's vision, we know, is eternal and not obstructed by the barrier of time. There is no past or future in God. Eternity is, as it were, a single present moment, the eternal *now* as the theologians describe it. Even though thousands of years were to elapse between the fall of Adam and the historical event of the Crucifixion, the eternal Father, immediately on decreeing to send his Son—*the seed of the woman*—to save mankind, saw in his prevision, the dead Christ on the cross, who had atoned by the shedding of his own blood, not the blood of victims, for the injury done to the divine majesty by Adam's sin and by the sins of mankind . . . *Christ making peace through the blood of his cross* (Col. 1 : 20).

In *Romans* (3 : 25–26) St. Paul represents God, on promising Adam a Redeemer, as placing before himself the dead Christ, a *propitiation or atonement for all who believe*, as a perpetual reminder that full atonement had been made for sin; that Christ had fulfilled, by shedding the last drop of his blood, the mission concerning sin on which God had sent him into the world (Ros. 8 : 4); that Christ, having fulfilled his contract so to speak, divine justice binds God to accept Christ's sacrifice as atonement for the sins of mankind; that, as Christ had paid the ransom for the sins of men, divine justice binds God to release from the slavery of sin those whom Christ has ransomed, those namely who are united with him by faith.

The primacy of Christ

This is St. Paul's way of conveying to our minds a great truth, namely the primacy of Christ in the economy of redemption— all sins are forgiven on the authority of Christ; without Christ's authority no sin can be forgiven. Analogy or comparison between things human and divine is always of its nature defective. We can, perhaps, understand St. Paul's thought the better for an illustration from a human court of justice. The image of the ruling power, or some symbol of state authority, is set up in a court of justice as a reminder of the judge's authority to dispense justice. The crucified Christ, whom St. Paul represents God as setting before himself, is his warrant for forgiving sin and for absolving the sinner *who belongs to Christ by faith*.

It is by faith in Christ ($\delta\iota\grave{\alpha}$ $\pi\acute{\iota}\sigma\tau\epsilon\omega s$ 3 : 24) the sinner avails himself of Christ's sacrifice. Faith hands the sinner over to Jesus, identifies his case with that of Jesus, so that if God rejects him he is rejecting Jesus. This is the sinner's sole claim against God. It is here divine justice intervenes on his behalf. He can do nothing of himself to merit justification. The gift of faith in Jesus is a gratuitous gift of God. The forgiveness of his sins is due solely to the merits of Christ, who paid the price of redemption.

Christ's death on the cross atoned for the sins of all time, those committed before Christ and those committed in the Christian era. God, by setting before himself the crucified Christ from the moment he promised a Redeemer, proves to all who may question it, that God *is himself just* (3 : 26) in accepting Christ's sacrifice of atonement; *and just in forgiving the sinner who belongs to Christ by faith*, whose ransom Christ has paid.

The justice of God in question in verse 25 ($\delta\iota\kappa\alpha\iota\sigma\sigma\acute{\upsilon}\nu\eta$) is retributive justice, that which gives each one his due—acceptance by God of Christ's sacrifice of atonement for the injury done to God's majesty by sin, and forgiveness of *the sinner belonging to Christ by faith*, because Christ has paid the price of his redemption. This is the justice of Acts 17 : 31, *He calls upon all men everywhere to repent because he has fixed a day, on which he will dispense justice on the world*, when each one will get his due. It is the justice men have in mind when they speak of a just God rewarding virtue or redressing wrongdoing.

This passage of *Romans* (3 : 25-26) has been called "one of the key passages of St. Paul's theology," "the epitome and mother idea of St. Paul's theology." "The divine, design" says Dom Columba Marmion, "is to constitute Christ the head of all the redeemed. . . . There is no thought more clearly expressed in the Epistles of St. Paul, none of which he is more convinced or that he places in higher relief. Read all his Epistles and you will see that he continually returns to this, making it almost all the substance of his doctrine."[1] The message of these verses is that without faith in Christ on the sinner's part even the omnipotent God cannot forgive sin; and, on the other hand, God is constrained by divine justice to receive into his friendship the sinner who is united with Christ by faith. The spiritual life of the Jews who profess to believe in God, but have rejected Christ, and put their faith in the works of the abrogated Law, is *a harvest for death* (Ros. 7 : 5).

The traditional version

The picture painted by St. Paul in *Romans* 3 : 25–26, illustrating the central and unique place that Christ holds in the economy of salvation, has been marred by the traditional translation and interpretation. The traditional version, which is said to date from the Reformation, is completely out of harmony with the context and does violence to the Greek original. It runs as follows: Christ (25) *whom God has set forth (on the cross) as a propitiatory sacrifice through the medium of faith, in his blood—so as to make manifest his justice, on account of the letting pass of former sins (26) in the period of God's patience—so as to make manifest his justice [I say] in the present time, [and to show] that he himself is just and that he justifies him who has faith in Jesus.*

The substance of this version as explained by the commentators, with variant details, is as follows: God set forth ($\pi\rho o\acute{\epsilon}\theta\epsilon\tau o$) Christ on the cross on the occasion of the Crucifixion, raised him up before the eyes of men as a propitiatory sacrifice, *in order to show forth at the present time the avenging justice of God in action, because of the letting pass ($\pi\acute{a}\rho\epsilon\sigma\iota\nu$) of former sins in the period of God's patience.* The justice of God which is displayed on the cross through Christ's sufferings is, according to this version, his *avenging vindictive justice*, also called *punitive justice*. The reason, it is said, of this display before the eyes of all in the present time (the Christian era), is "because God for a long time with marvellous patience allowed men's sins to go without punishment". Others of this school hold that the reason is, that God passed over men's sins committed before the Crucifixion, without remitting them.

[1] *Op. cit.*, p. 16.

In the second period, *the present time*, all the Christian period, men see by Christ's actual sufferings the magnitude of the ransom that God has demanded for sin and which Christ has paid—this being a clear proof of the greatness of the injury done to God by sin.

The cardinal error in this version is the meaning assigned to *justice* (δικαιοσύνη 3: 25). The sixteenth century translator, whoever he was, insisted that the justice in question is the avenging, vindictive justice of God. No parallel usage of the term is cited from the Epistles of St. Paul or from any other source. Some of the Reformers, assured of their own salvation, liked to emphasise the concept of an angry God demanding satisfaction for other men's iniquities. The commentators since that time have unquestioningly followed the trail. Everything in these two verses that naturally fails to harmonise with this concept of divine justice must be squared and adjusted to fit the issue. It becomes a tailoring process.

Others still hold that God had remitted such sins only provisionally, this being the particular meaning here of πάρεσις, *passing over*. All agree that God's purpose in setting forth Christ on the cross, as they interpret it, is to show forth *at the present time* the rigours of God's vindictive justice, that demanded such atonement from his own Son.

It is further maintained by these commentators that there have been two periods of "divine policy" towards sin. In the first period—the whole pre-Christian period—there was on God's part a πάρεσις of sin, whether this means toleration of sin without due chastisement, or passing over of sins without forgiveness or mere provisional forgiveness, the commentators are not agreed. This they maintain was the time of God's patience.

The sixteenth century translator ignored St. Paul's use of the verb προέθετο on the only two other occasions on which the word occurs in his writings. In *Romans* 1 : 13 the meaning clearly is *I put it before myself* (προεθέμην) *to visit you*, that is, a figurative usage describing a mental process. In *Ephesians* 1 : 9 St. Paul describes the goodly intent which God *put before himself* (προέθετο) in the case of Christ. The Latin exact equivalent in each case is *sibi proponere*. In the Septuagint προέθετο has exactly the same meaning: *violent men seek my life. They set not* (προέθεντο) *God before themselves* (Ps. 54: 5), *I set not before my eyes* (προεθέμην) *any*

base thing (Ps. 101 : 3). In the passage of *Romans* we are discussing,
St. Paul also uses the word figuratively, *God set before himself the
crucified Christ*. To help our limited comprehension St. Paul is
applying to the divine mind a human process. The sixteenth
century translator ignored the use of the middle voice and
assigned the word a literal signification, setting forth Christ on
the cross. There is worse to follow.

"Passing over" of sins

The expression πάρεσις ἁμαρτημάτων (v. 25) naturally and
normally means *remission of sins*, just as πάρεσις χρημάτων, which
occurs in the secular literature of St. Paul's time, means *remission of
debt*. But *remission of sins* would not suit the concept of *avenging,
vindictive justice*, and so had to be adjusted in meaning. It could
not be maintained that Christ's sufferings on the cross to show
forth God's vindictive justice, took place *because of the remission of
sins* as the Greek text demands. Forgiveness of sin implies that the
divine wrath has been propitiated. The adjusted meaning of the
term is *passing over of sins*. Then the position is reached, that
Christ's sufferings on the cross took place to show forth to men
God's vindictive justice *because of the passing over of sins formerly
committed*. We are told that no dreadful punishment for sin
reflecting even slightly its guilt,—except the Deluge,—was
inflicted by God for sins in the pre-Christian period; so that "it
might have seemed as if God took little heed of sin."

Now, every Christian schoolboy knows that Christ died on the
cross because of men's sins, not because God passed over men's
sins, whatever the nature of the *passing over*. Even a cursory
reading of the Old Testament will show that God in his dealings
with his chosen people never let sin go unpunished . . . *who
renderest the iniquity of the fathers to the children and to the grand-
children unto the third and the fourth generation* (Exod. 34 : 7)
And speaking of the gentiles, St. Paul says that *the wrath of God
manifests itself from heaven against every impiety and wickedness
of men who maliciously suppress the truth concerning God* (Ros. 1, 18)
There seems to be no evidence whatever at any time, for the
suggestion that "it might have seemed as if God took little
heed of sin." And how, may we ask, were those who witnessed
the Crucifixion to know that Christ's sufferings on the cross
took place because God *had passed over sins formerly committed*

The traditional version is, *to make manifest his avenging justice on account of the letting pass of former sins*. According to this version, it was God's action *in letting former sins pass*, and not man's action in committing sin, that caused the Crucifixion. It is absurd.

There is another explanation of πάρεσις ἁμαρτημάτων (v. 25), equally invalid. A distinction is drawn between πάρεσις and ἄφεσις ἁμαρτημάτων. The term ἄφεσις is said to connote absolute, definitive remission of sin such as we have in the Christian era; while πάρεσις indicates some sort of provisional remission, it being claimed that sins were "held in abeyance" until the Crucifixion actually occurred. The remission then, according to this theory, was provisional on the actual occurrence of the Crucifixion, and became definitive only when the Crucifixion took place, something in the nature of a suspensory sentence in our courts of justice,— the implication being that before the Crucifixion sin could not be definitively forgiven because God's avenging justice had not been propitiated.

The Israelites under the Mosaic Law understood that their sins were forgiven definitively not provisionally. *Blot out my iniquities*, prays the Psalmist, *wash me wholly from my guilt and cleanse me of my sins . . . that I may become wholly clean . . . that I may become whiter than snow* (Ps. 51 : 4–9). *Bless God who has forgiven all my iniquities . . . As far as the East is from the West he has removed all our sins from us* (Ps. 103 : 3–12). The sinner may feel confident that God *hurls into the depth of the sea all his sins* (Mich. 7 : 19), where they disappear for ever. Ezechiel, admonishing his people to strive for a new heart and a new spirit, says that *all the sins which the sinner committed shall no longer be remembered* (Ezech. 18 : 22). The prophet Nathan assured David that his sin was forgiven, "taken away" (2 Kgs. 12 : 13). Very frequently during Christ's public life we hear the sentence pronounced by him *thy sins are forgiven thee*. The Greek leaves no doubt that the action has been completed. Was this only provisional remission of sin? Christ lived under the Law, and observed its *every jot and tittle*. If sins were only provisionally forgiven under the Law, the correct form of the sentence would be *thy sins will be forgiven thee*.

It is just as arbitrary to claim that there is a real distinction between the Greek forms πάρεσις and ἄφεσις in relation to the remission of sin, as to suggest a real distinction between the

English forms *remission* and *forgiveness*. The correct translation of πάρεσις ἁμαρτημάτων in Romans 3 : 25 is *remission of sins*, without qualification. The correct Latin version is that of the Vulgate *remissio peccatorum* not *praetermissio* as the commentators suggest. We have proof of this in the very next verse (26). It is impossible to make sense of verse 26 unless the clause *in remission of sins* διὰ τὴν πάρεσιν ἁμαρτημάτων is supplied from the preceding verse. The traditional version *so as to make manifest his justice* [*I say*] *in the present time* is a mere repetition of the statement in verse 25. Repetition is certainly no feature of St. Paul's writings. He was "a saint in a hurry" where his writings are concerned. Ellipsis is much more characteristic of him. There is no repetition in verse 26. There is a clear contrast between *the remission of sins committed before Christ* and *remission of sins at the present time*. Commentators will surely not suggest that the remission of sins at the present time is not definitive. St. Paul represents God as setting before himself immediately on his promise of a Redeemer, the dead Christ who has shed his blood, a victim of propitiation for all who believe in him, God's purpose in doing so, being to show forth his justice (δικαιοσύνη) in remitting sins committed before Christ's coming, because of Christ's atonement. Then God is represented as looking *forward* (πρός) to the future, to the Christian period. Literally, the clause runs, *towards the proof of his justice* [*in remitting sins*] *at the present time*.

The principle of remission of sin at all periods in man's history remains the same, namely faith in the promised Redeemer, *the seed of the woman*. St. Paul is here emphasising God's acknowledgement, as in justice due, of Christ's atonement; not God's showing forth of his avenging justice, which has been already propitiated by Christ's atonement on the cross, *a propitiation by virtue of the shedding of his own blood*.

In the latter part of verse 26 the traditional version, dating we are told from the sixteenth century, is guilty of a sheer and obvious mistranslation. It runs thus, to *show that he himself* (God) *is just, and that he justifies him who has faith in Jesus*. Grammatically, according to the Greek of St. Paul, it should run thus, *to show that he himself is just and just in justifying him who has faith in Jesus*. The translator alters the sense by construing the participle δικαιοῦντα as if it were an infinitive. The mistranslation, inadvertent of course, saved the translator from a veritable impasse.

How could it be said that God showed forth his avenging, vindictive justice in forgiving the sinner? Some of the commentators have proved themselves equal even to this situation. The justice in question, which in verse 25 was *avenging vindictive justice*, now becomes "moral perfection in general," sometimes called "justice," sometimes "holiness". Similarly *forgiveness of sin* can mean *passing over of sin* without forgiveness or without punishment, or merely provisional forgiveness. It is certainly no easy task to grapple with this Proteus.

It has been said, and said correctly, that these two verses (Romans 3 : 25–26) are the "epitome and mother idea of St. Paul's theology". How is this significance seen in the traditional interpretation? *God set forth Christ on the cross to show forth in the present time* (during the Christian era) *his avenging, vindictive justice. . . .* What good news is there here for mankind? The gospel, as the Greek word implies, is a record of good news. Surely this was not the burden of St. Paul's teaching. It is, of course, salutary to realise the enormity of sin that cost such a price, and the crucifix itself is a constant reminder of the price of man's redemption. But it is much more consoling for the sinner to realise that Christ by his sufferings and death on the cross fully atoned for the injury done by sin to God's majesty: that Christ's sufferings and death have wiped out the handwriting against mankind; that justice—the justice that gives each one his due—demands that God will acknowledge Christ's sacrifice and accept his atonement; that justice, furthermore, demands that God will forgive the sinner who is incorporated in Christ by faith, whose ransom Christ has paid; that rejection by God of the sinner united with Christ would be tantamount to rejection of Christ. This certainly was good news for mankind, and this was the message St. Paul preached—the primacy of Christ in the economy of salvation.

In *Romans* 3 : 23–24, the two verses immediately preceding the passage under discussion, the need for forgiveness is stressed and the process of forgiveness ($\delta\iota\kappa\alpha\iota o\acute{\upsilon}\mu\epsilon\nu o\iota$) is represented as a free gift through God's love. In the picture painted by St. Paul the ransom has been paid and atonement made, and acceptance by God, as in justice due, acknowledged. The sufferings of Christ have ended, and are not seen in operation, as traditional commentators maintain. In this atmosphere that breathes the love and mercy of God for the sinner there is no place for the discordant note of avenging, vindictive justice. Surely St. Paul did not mean to convey that the lesson of the crucifix during the Christian era is that of an angry God.

Justification a free gift

Emphasis is laid on the gratuitousness of God's gift of justification because the Jews, for whose immediate instruction St. Paul was writing, professed that they could win salvation by performing the works of the Mosaic Law—*the justification of their own*, not the justification which God gives through faith in Christ (Ros. 10 : 4). The sinner, of course, must co-operate with God's free gift of grace. Faith in Christ implies this. He is free to reject it. And failure to ask for it is equivalent to rejection. The redemption or ransom, which Christ paid in his own person, is the one and only means at God's disposal for forgiving sins. Christ is the one and only Mediator between God and man. The merits of Christ's sacrifice were available for the sinner united with Christ, from the moment God promised Adam, and through him the human race, a Redeemer; and will remain available for all time. To show that divine justice binds him to acknowledge the atonement of Christ and binds him to forgive the sinner, whose ransom Christ has paid, St. Paul represents God as placing before his mind's eye, from the moment he promised a Redeemer, the figure of the dead Christ who was both an atonement and a redemption by *virtue of the shedding of his own blood.*

The traditional interpretation completely misses the significance of this key passage in St. Paul's Epistle to the Romans. The traditional interpretation lays the emphasis not on forgiveness of sin, but on "passing over" of sins because the anger of God has not been appeased; and the message of the Cross is God's avenging, vindictive justice. This was not the Christianity St. Paul preached. It is not true to St. Paul's Greek. This interpretation savours of Calvinism. One wonders how it ever came to be accepted. One wonders, also, what false notion of loyalty prompts commentators to defend it even now. It is devoid of merit on any score.

For all men have sinned and have forfeited the glory of God, being justified as a free gift through God's love by means of the Redemption that is in Christ Jesus. Whom God set before himself—an atonement for those who believe in him, by virtue of the shedding of his own blood—*as proof of God's justice in forgiving through his forbearance sins committed before Christ; to be the proof of his justice* [*in forgiving sins*] *at the present time; proving that God is himself just* (in accepting Christ's atonement), *and just in forgiving the sinner who belongs to Jesus through faith* (whose ransom Christ has paid). *Romans* 3 : 23–26.

Chapter Four

THE CASE OF ABRAHAM

HAVING established that in the forgiveness of sin all authority rests with Jesus, St. Paul asks *where then is there room for boasting?* (Ros. 3 : 27). There is no room for the boasting of the Jews that they could save themselves by the works of the Mosaic Law, which was now abrogated. The vast majority of the Jewish nation still placed their faith in the Law. They were the children of Abraham, they claimed; circumcision and the Law surely guaranteed them the fulfilment of the promises made to their father Abraham. They refused to believe in *justification through faith in Christ without reference to the Law.* Was Abraham not the founder of the Jewish race and . . . were the Jews not the inheritors of the promises made to Abraham? They surely were the children of the kingdom.

The encounter between Christ and the Jews, related in the eighth chapter of St. John's gospel, illustrates the presumption of the Jews in their claiming to be Abraham's children. That surely was title sufficient for salvation. *If you continue,* said Jesus, *faithful to my word you are my disciples in earnest, and you will know the truth and the truth will set you free* (Jn. 8 : 32–33). They indignantly replied that they were the children of Abraham and had never been enslaved to any one. *Abraham is our father.* Jesus replied: *If you are Abraham's true children, it is for you to follow Abraham's example; as it is, you are designing to kill me who told you the truth I have heard from God. This Abraham did not do.* When Jesus said that the man who kept his word would not see death for eternity, the Jews retorted: *Art thou greater than our father Abraham? He is dead.* Then Jesus said, *Abraham your father exulted in the thought of seeing my day. He saw it and rejoiced*

54

(Jn. 8 : 57). Abraham's faith in God, therefore, implied faith in Christ and it was through his faith in Christ that Abraham was justified.

Immediately after describing how justification is possible only through union with Christ by faith, St. Paul devotes a whole chapter to the case of Abraham. He wished to correct the false notion of the Jews that because they were the descendants of Abraham they were his children, and heirs to the promises made to him. When John saw Pharisees and Sadducees approaching his baptism, he ordered them *to yield the acceptable fruit of penance. Do not presume to say to yourselves, "we have Abraham for our father". God has power to raise up children to Abraham out of these very stones* (Mt. 3 : 8–9). Carnal descent from Abraham as indicated by circumcision, does not prove kinship with Abraham in the sense that matters before God. The children of Abraham are the children of Abraham's faith, irrespective of race or origin.

The call of Abraham

Abraham, whose date may be assigned with much probability to the second half of the eighteenth century B.C., lived at Haran in Mesopotamia. He received a call from God: *Leave your country, your relatives and your father's house, for the land that I will show you. I will make a great nation of you. . . . In you shall all nations of the earth be blessed* (Gen. 12 : 1–3). While God's call was an extraordinary grace for Abraham, it also implied great sacrifices,— leaving his country and friends and departing into the unknown. Such was Abraham's faith in God that he obeyed with alacrity. God promised him that a great people would descend from him. But Abraham was childless, and his wife Sara sterile; and both were now well advanced in years. Abraham, in his new home, gained wealth and prestige but remained childless. Again God promised him that his descendants would be as numerous as the stars of the heavens (Gen. 15 : 5). Abraham believed God's promise, although the natural signs were all set in the opposite direction. Abraham, as Paul says, *hoped against hope.*

When finally Abraham was told by heavenly messengers that his wife Sara, who was now ninety years of age, would bear him a son within a year, Sara who overheard the conversation laughed, the idea seemed so fantastic. But Abraham's faith in God remained unshaken. The child Isaac was born as promised, and grew up to be strong enough to carry the wood for the altar on which his father meant to sacrifice him, for so God had ordered him: *Take thy only begotten son Isaac whom thou lovest . . . and offer him for a holocaust upon one of the mountains which I will show thee* (Gen. 22 : 2). This was the supreme test of Abraham's faith— he was ordered by God to put to death the child whom he loved, on whom alone the fulfilment of the promises depended. Again, Abraham's faith stood the test. He proceeded to obey without question, when God directly intervened to save the boy.

Abraham's faith

Abraham's unfaltering faith in God was the source of all his greatness. God's grace and friendship were added. *Abraham believed in God and it was accredited to him for justification* (Ros. 3 : 3). The very form of the statement shows that there was no equality between the service given and the return. A man owes his neighbour a large sum of money. If the debtor makes a token payment of a trifling sum, the neighbour may generously accredit him the whole debt. There is this difference however, in Abraham's case. His faith, for which he was accredited justification, was itself a free gift from God. Nothing that Abraham could himself do, could merit God's bounty. The promise that from Abraham the Redeemer would descend—for so the promise was always interpreted—but crowned the gift of faith that Abraham had already received. The promise was absolute. There was no contract of *do ut des*. The promise was in no way conditioned or qualified by the giving of the Law to Moses some four hundred years subsequently. It was only after the promise that God imposed circumcision as an obligation on the household of Abraham, as a seal or sign of the promise (Ros. 4 : 11).

The Jews maintained that as descendants of Abraham, with the distinguishing marks of circumcision and possession of the Mosaic Law, they and they alone were heirs to the promise. The Law was sufficient guarantee of their right to the inheritance. St. Paul replies: *For it was not through the Law the promise was made to Abraham or to his seed, that he was to be the heir of the world, but through faith which brings justification. For if it was a case of heirs through observance of the Law, then Abraham's faith has been voided and the promise nullified* (4 : 13–14). It was admitted on all sides that the Law had not been observed. St. Peter at the

Council of Jerusalem protested against the effort to impose on the disciples *a yoke which neither we nor our fathers have been able to bear* (Ac. 15 : 11). *Therefore the promise was given as a result of faith—in which case (ἵνα) as a free gift—showing that the promise was guaranteed for the descendants of Abraham through faith* (Ros. 4 : 16).

Faith then is the hallmark of Abraham's children, faith in God and in Christ whom the gospel reveals as the Son of God and the promised Redeemer, whose day Abraham exulted to see. Jew and gentile, provided only they have faith, are Abraham's children. There was point, therefore, in the Baptist's remark to the Pharisees and Sadducees that *God could raise up children to Abraham from these stones.* If God only clothed the stones in flesh and blood and endowed these newly formed men with the gift of faith, they would be more truly children of Abraham than the Jews who rejected Christ, and thus renounced Abraham's faith and lost the inheritance of the kingdom of God.

The privileges given to Abraham were given *in return for* ("*over against*") *what he believed* (κατέναντι οὗ ἐπίστευσεν),[1] *namely that God it is who gives life to the dead just as* (καὶ) *he calls into being things not in being* (Ros. 4 : 17). It was through God's direct intervention, in the first instance, that Isaac the child of promise came into being; and, although all the natural signs were set against it, Abraham's faith never wavered in God's omnipotence and his fidelity to his promise. When ordered by God to put the child to death, Abraham's faith again assured him that even in such seemingly impossible circumstances *God is also able to accomplish what was promised* (4 : 21); that, just as in the first instance God miraculously called Isaac into being, so now also even though his father, at God's command, sacrifices the child's life, God can and will restore him to life. . . . *God it is who gives life to the dead.*

Abraham's faith served as the source of redemption and salvation for all mankind. The gospel now reveals that Christ was the *seed of Abraham* who was to bring blessing to all mankind. The doctrine of justification by faith in Christ supersedes the old distinction between Jew and gentile based on circumcision. Grace was given to Abraham, not primarily for his own advantage

---

[1]The relative οὗ is genitive by attraction. The following clause is genitive in opposition to οὗ.

(4; 23) or the advantage of his race, but for the sake of all mankind. Abraham's call did not imply that God was abandoning the nations of the earth, but that he was preparing for them the way of salvation. Christ himself made it plain on one occasion that blood relationship did not count in the kingdom he was establishing. It was during his Galilean ministry when his Mother and his brethren called at a house where he was preaching and asked to see him. When the message was conveyed to Jesus that his Mother and his brethren wished to see him, stretching his hand towards his disciples he said: *See my mother and my brothers. Whoever does the will of my Father in heaven is my brother and my sister and my mother* (Matt. 12 : 49–50). Christ the promised Messias, the descendant of Abraham, like Abraham himself, does not belong to the Jews or to any section of mankind. He belongs to the whole human race.

Chapter Five

FAITH ALONE?

THERE is a further question in connexion with justification by faith—is it "faith alone" as some of the Reformers would have it? There is no mention any place in the Scriptures of "faith alone". Is there, in fact, any reality corresponding to this formula? In the ordinary affairs of life the faith in a man or cause that is confined to mere profession or lip service, is considered of poor account. Faith that fails to express itself in action, where action is demanded, must be regarded as something devitalised. Abraham is the classical instance of justification by faith. Yet God, speaking to Isaac, says: *I will multiply thy seed like the stars of heaven ... and in thy seed shall all the nations of the earth be blessed, because Abraham obeyed my voice and kept my precepts and commandments, and observed my ceremonies and laws* (Gen. 26 : 4–5). The test of Abraham's faith was obedience to God's commandments. His faith expressed itself in action.

Justification by faith implies a willingness on the part of the sinner to conform to the requirements of the law under which he lives. The man depending for his salvation on the Natural Law is forgiven his sins through faith in the promised Redeemer. The forgiveness of sin always implies sorrow for sin and the resolve to avoid it,—these two conditions being naturally fundamental to the forgiveness of any crime.

Those who lived under the Mosaic Law were bound in addition to carry out the precepts of the Law. *He who does the justice of the Law shall live thereby* (Ros. 10 : 5). Doing the *justice of the Law* means carrying out the will of the Lawgiver. Faith in the promised Redeemer was the spirit or soul of the Mosaic Law.

For those living under the New Dispensation, faith in the

Redeemer Christ implies sorrow for sin and the resolve to avoid it, and in addition at least a willingness to receive the sacrament of baptism; while reception of baptism implies a willingness to submit to the discipline of the Church to which Christ entrusted the power committed to him by the Father, and of which baptism confers membership. In every case faith in the Redeemer, which is essential for justification, implies a readiness to conform to the requirements of the law under which the sinner lives. Works are the complement or corollary of faith.

Faith and works

In the Epistles of St. Paul there is no opposition between faith and works, taking these terms in their ordinarily accepted sense. On the judgement day *God will render to each one in accordance with his works* (Ros. 2 : 6). *It is not the hearers of a law who are just in God's sight, but the doers of a law who will be justified on the day when God will judge the secret lives of men* (Ros. 2 : 13, 16). In the New Dispensation *there is no virtue in circumcision or in the want of it; it is keeping the commandments of God that counts* (1 Cor. 7 : 19).

In the Epistles, however, the term *faith* very frequently means faith in Christ, and the term *works* means the works of the abrogated Mosaic Law; and between these two concepts there is violent opposition. The Jews professed faith in God, but for the most part rejected Christ and sought their justification through the works of the Law. The Law abrogated by the death of Christ became the implacable enemy of Christ and entered the list on the side of sin (Ros. 5 : 20). The Law that was instituted by God to make of Israel *a priestly kingdom and a holy nation* now became *a law of sin and death* (8 : 2). In this sense, and in this sense only, is there opposition in the writings of St. Paul between faith and works.

Nobody reading the Epistle to the Romans will argue that St. Paul ignores works in the quest of salvation. *With our sins forgiven us, then, through faith, let us remain at peace with God through Our Lord Jesus Christ, through whom we have attained access to the grace in which we stand* (Ros. 5 : 1–2). The sinner who has died to sin in baptism through sharing mystically in the death of Christ, is exhorted to live the new life of the spirit, that is the life of grace, which mystic resurrection with Christ implies.

Baptism means the death of the old man of sin—*life in the flesh*—
and judicial liberation (δεδικαίωται 6 : 7) from slavery to sin.
St. Paul reminds his audience that they are no longer living in
the regime of the abrogated Mosaic Law which they have
abandoned, where through absence of grace sin held absolute
sway (7 : 14ff.), but under the regime of grace (5 : 14), and warns
them of the necessity of co-operating with grace in the performance
of good works. *Now make your members slaves to justice and
holiness* (6 : 19). Christians, in order to be glorified with Christ,
must suffer with Christ (8 : 17). They are exhorted to offer up
their bodies as a living sacrifice (12 : 1). Those who love God,
that is, keep God's commandments, are assured of reaching the
goal of salvation, no matter what the course of events. *For we
know that for those who love God all things co-operate for good* (8:28).

God's plan for the elect

Those who love God are here identified by St. Paul with those
who are in the category of *the called* (κλητοί) in God's plan
(πρόθεσις) for the salvation of the elect. According to St. Paul
God drew up from eternity, before creation, a plan for the elect,
just as an architect makes beforehand a plan of his proposed
building, working out each detail of his edifice. God's purpose,
says St. Paul, in drawing up this plan was in preparation for the
coming of Christ, *so that Christ would be the first born of many
brethren* (Ros. 8 : 29) who would share his glory for eternity.
*Father, I will that where I am, there also those whom thou hast
given me may be with me* (Jn. 17 : 24),—that is, *co-heirs of Christ*.

On what principle were those destined to be co-heirs of Christ,
selected by God when he was drawing up his plan before creation?
Did God arbitrarily select A B and C and reject D and E? So the
Calvinists say. Certain souls are saved from the beginning and
others are marked off for perdition, and try as they may, they
cannot avoid it. In the plan mentioned by St. Paul in *Romans*
8 : 29–30 there is no reference whatever to those who fail in the
struggle for salvation. He is speaking only of the elect chosen to
be Christ's brethren and co-heirs; but the manner of their election
explains the fate of the lost.

*We know all things co-operate for good for those who love God,
being those called in his plan. Because those whom he knew from
eternity conformed to the image of his Son, he also marked off from*

eternity, so that Christ would be the first born among many brethren. Those whom he marked off from eternity he also called. Those whom he called he also justified. Those whom he justified, he also glorified (Ros. 8 : 29–30).

All events that have happened or will happen are always present to the eye of God. The day will come when the human race will cease to exist and mankind will have received at the hands of God the reward or punishment for eternity that their lives on earth merited. The fate of souls at the end of the world is known to God from eternity, some in glory *conformed to the image of his Son;* others,—but of these St. Paul makes no mention. The divine plan is concerned only with the elect. *Those whom he knew from eternity conformed to the image of his own Son, he also marked off from eternity*. Those alone were the subject of his plan drawn up from eternity before creation, that Christ might have many brethren in glory. The souls of the just, from Adam to the last human being who will be born, are included in this plan, which will be translated into action until the end of time. The subjects of the plan were chosen on their merits, *those whom God knew in glory*. Before creation God saw the souls of the just in glory, and these souls were chosen to be the brethren of Christ.

Post praevisam gloriam

St. Paul's translators, however, have not done him justice here. Beginning with the Vulgate they represent him as saying that God marked off or predestined certain souls *to be conformed* to the image of his Son, as if the Greek here was σνμμόρφους εἶναι (29). The Vulgate reads *conformes fieri, to be made conformed*. Then naturally a controversy arose concerning the principle on which God made his choice. Was it before or after seeing the merits of those chosen? The Greek makes it plain that the choice was made after seeing them in glory, *those whom he knew from eternity conformed. . . .*

St. Paul, then, does not represent God as making his choice on any arbitrary principle. There is no suggestion that certain souls are saved and others not saved independently of any part these souls could play in the course of life. The choice was made not beforehand, but only when the soul had won its honours in the contest and had already been glorified, as seen by God from

eternity before creation. The souls selected for God's plan as
indicated by St. Paul, to be Christ's brethren, are those who,
from Adam to the last born of the human race, whether under the
Natural Law, the Mosaic Law or the New Dispensation had, by
loving God, that is by keeping God's commandments, secured
salvation.

In the plan as outlined by St. Paul there are four stages: the
souls who are to be the subject of the plan are marked off or
predestined (προώρισεν); then in succession they are called
(ἐκάλεσεν), justified (ἐδικαίωσεν), and glorified (ἐδόξασεν). It will
be noted that the past tense is used concerning each operation as
if already accomplished, although when this plan was drawn up
by God, no soul had yet been created. The past tense can be
explained only on the assumption that God finished off each
detail of his plan, as an architect completes on paper the various
parts of his proposed building. Some commentators explain the
past tense as prophetic past, that is viewing the future as already
having happened. In prophetic literature the past tense is so used
where the prophet visualises the future event as having already
occurred, so certain is it of accomplishment. The Epistles of
St. Paul, however, are not prophetic literature. St. Paul is not
speaking here as a prophet.

When God promised Adam a Redeemer, he saw in that instant
the figure of the dead Christ on the cross, pleading as in justice
due to his sacrifice, for the forgiveness of sinners united with
him by faith (Ros. 3 : 25). The Greek word προέθετο is used by
St. Paul to describe God putting before himself the figure of the
dead Christ. The term πρόθεσις, describing God's plan for the
elect, is a derivative substantive, from the same verb (προτίθημι)
and expressing the same idea—God *setting before himself* the plan
or salvation of those who would be Christ's brethren in glory.
These processes applied by St. Paul to the divine mind are
intended to assist our limited comprehension. In *Romans* 3 : 25
the lesson to be learned is the essential primacy of Christ in the
divine scheme of salvation. In chapter 8 : 29–30 the sinner is
reminded of the part he must play to secure salvation. He must
suffer with Christ to be glorified with Christ (8 : 18). But no
matter what happens, whether one's lot is victory or defeat in the
immediate struggle, the soul that loves God need never be
perturbed for the final issue. Those who love God are *the called*

in God's plan for the elect (Ros. 8 : 28). Their names are written in the Book of Life. Loving God means keeping the commandments of God (Mt. 7 : 21).

There is nothing in St. Paul's Epistle to the Romans to suggest that "faith alone" is sufficient for salvation. Those who on the Day of Resurrection will be conformed to the image of the risen Christ will be those whose faith has expressed itself in the love of God.

Chapter Six

JUSTIFICATION UNDER THE NATURAL LAW

THE sin of Paradise was a sin of disobedience due to pride. Adam received for himself and his race the grace that made of him a child of God. He and his wife Eve enjoyed wonderful blessings, the intimate friendship of God their creator and benefactor, bodily immortality and immunity from suffering, sorrow, pain and disease—on one condition, however, that they abstain from eating of *the tree of knowledge. For on that day when you eat of it you must die* (Gen. 2 : 16–17).

The tempter envied them their happiness and urged them to disobey God, *No, you will not die . . . you will be like God knowing good and evil* (Gen. 3 : 5). The threatened punishment fell upon them. They were doomed to die. *Through sin death has come into the world* (Ros. 5 : 12). The author of the Book of Wisdom says that *through the envy of the devil death has come into the world* (2 : 24). The apostle John calls the devil *a murderer from the beginning* (Jn. 8 : 44) and *the old serpent who betrayed the whole world* (Apoc. 12 : 9).

A Redeemer promised

By delaying the execution of the death sentence, God granted our first parents an opportunity to do penance and regain his friendship. They were driven from the bliss of Paradise conscious of having forfeited the *glory of God*, but they were not abandoned to despair. A Redeemer was promised them, *the seed of the woman who would crush the serpent's head* (Gen. 3 : 15). *By hope we were saved* (Ros. 8 : 24) says St. Paul. God's mercy followed close on the heels of his justice. The tempter had brought disaster on mankind, but his reign would also come to an end. *I will cause*

enmity between you and the woman, between your seed and her seed.
This was the sentence of condemnation of sin, which would one
day be executed on the Cross through the death of the Redeemer
in his sinless human nature (Ros. 8 : 5). But the efficacy of this
condemnation of sin became immediately available for those who
were united through faith with the promised Redeemer. When
Adam's eldest son Cain, instigated by jealousy, was contemplating
the murder of his brother Abel, God spoke to Cain, *why art thou
angry? and why is thy countenance fallen? If thou do well, shalt thou
not receive? but if ill, shall sin not forthwith be present at the door?
but the lust thereof shall be under thee and thou shalt have dominion
over it* (Gen. 4 : 6–7). Through union, therefore, by faith with
the promised *seed of the woman*, mankind from the beginning was
in a position to resist sin. And if he forfeited God's grace by
committing sin, man was able to recover it through faith in the
promised Redeemer (Ros. 3 : 26).

This good news to our first parents of a Redeemer to come, the
protoevangel as it is called, is the first joyful message of forgiveness
from sin. St. Paul represents, as we shall see, that this hope of
redemption is the inheritance of every child of Adam as surely
as he has inherited the consequences of Adam's sin. Memories of
a lost Paradise linger in every soul. St. Paul also represents that
every human soul has an intimation that it is the child of God.

Besides this instinctive intimation of their origin and destiny,
what means are at the disposal of man, living under the Natural
Law without any direct revelation, of discovering the true God
and the manner of worshipping him? In Paradise Adam and Eve
enjoyed God's love in a most special measure. Their intimacy with
God was greater than that of any prophet in subsequent times, and
their knowledge of God more profound. Time and distance
dimmed this knowledge in their descendants. But every man of
average intellectual capacity is endowed with the faculty of
discovering the true God, and the law that governs man's relations
with God is inscribed in each man's heart (Ros. 2 : 15).

The means of knowing God

According to St. Paul, evidence for knowledge of God is in
their midst for all men to see. God himself put the visible evidence
there for them (Ros. 1 : 19). Man need but consider the order,
the greatness and grandeur of the universe to make him think of

God and praise him. *The heavens show forth the glory of God, and the firmament declares the work of his hands* (Ps. 19 : 2). The works of creation, the starry heavens, the succession of day and night, the regular recurrence of the seasons, the earth and its fruits, all proclaim a Creator supreme and beneficent. God can be seen in the world of nature. *His attributes which are not visible to the eye*, namely his omnipotence and divinity are clearly visible to the human intellect reflecting on his *operations* (ποιήματα) since the creation of the world (Ros. 1 : 20).

There is a clear distinction drawn here between the attributes of God which are visible in creation and those which are visible only to the mind of man (νοούμενα). What are these *operations* which supply the human intellect with the means of discovering God's omnipotence and divinity? This passage of St. Paul's *Romans* bears a close affinity with passages in the Book of Wisdom: *But all men are vain in whom there is not the knowledge of God, and who by these good things that are seen could not understand him that is, neither by attending to the works have acknowledged who was the workman* (Wis. 13 : 1). This is the evidence which is plain to be seen (φανερόν 1 : 19). God's divinity and omnipotence are on a different footing. Holiness is the great attribute of divinity, and opposition to sin is the first requisite of holiness. *Who will convict me of sin?* said Christ (Jn. 8 : 46).

And God seeing that the wickedness of man was great on the earth . . . it repented him that he had made man on the earth (Gen. 6 : 5–6). Tradition of the Deluge was universal in the early history of the world. The destruction by fire of Sodom and Gomorrha conveyed the same lesson of God's abomination of sin. The miracles in Egypt in connexion with the liberation of the Israelites, when God executed *judgement over all the gods of Egypt*, revealed in a vivid manner God's power, his supremacy over the mighty Pharaoh and his dominion over the powers of nature. *For thou showest thy power when men will not believe thee to be absolute in power, and thou convincest the boldness of them that know thee not* (Wm. 12 : 17).

The Natural Law

It can be demonstrated then, according to St. Paul, by human observation and human reason that a Supreme Deity exists, Creator of the world on whom all things depend, who will reward the good and punish the wicked. Human reason demands that he be worshipped as befits God, and points to duties towards God and our fellowmen which form what is known as the Natural Law, a law written in each man's conscience (Ros. 2 : 14), which is to be his sole guide in the work of salvation. The tendency to idolatry was, however, always strong even amongst God's chosen people, who enjoyed special revelation. The struggle of the prophets from Moses to the close of the exile was a struggle against the tendency to worship idols. *It has ever been the same since the day I rescued them from Egypt; me they will ever be forsaking, to worship other gods* (1 Kgs. 8 : 8). St. Paul says that *the anger of God is revealed from heaven against every impiety and wickedness of men who maliciously suppress the truth concerning God* (Ros. 1 : 18). Idolatry was the fruitful source of moral degradation: *That is why God abandoned their lustful hearts to the filthy practices of dishonouring their own bodies among themselves* (Ros. 1 : 24). It is to be inferred that God's mercy, on the other hand, will be extended to those whose guilt in the worship of the true God will be extenuated by ignorance or weakness as distinct from malice.

The existence of the Natural Law in men's hearts is revealed, St. Paul says, when *gentiles who have no (written) law, instinctively* (φύσει) *perform duties which the (Mosaic) Law prescribes* (Ros. 2 : 15), precepts, that is, of the Natural Law which are embodied in the written code of the Mosaic Law. *Their conscience also,* he says, *bears witness thereto and their arguments among themselves condemning or defending a proposition* (Ros. 2 : 15). The gentile conscience is revealed in history and literature. The *Agamemnon* of Aeschylus, for instance, illustrates the sharp reaction of the pagan conscience to murder and adultery; while in the Dialogues of Plato theological and moral questions of great moment are debated.

In listing the catalogue of gentile sins (Ros. 1 : 24–32) Paul says that the gentiles *knew the decree of God, that those who do such things are worthy of death.* It is incorrect, therefore, to state that "outside the Mosaic Law the sense of sin is dead", as exegetes sometimes state when commenting on *Romans* 7 : 8. Conscience of right and wrong in the gentiles implies their moral obligations to God and their neighbours, in the light of such knowledge as the Natural Law reveals.

The Spirit bears witness . . .

Reason is unable to discover anything with certainty of the intimate life of the Supreme Being. The divine life appears to natural reason to be infinitely distant, God dwelling far off *in light inaccessible*. Revelation teaches of the paternity of God. God is a father, with a father's love and solicitude for his children. St. Paul implies that every human soul has an intimation of being God's child. *The Spirit bears witness along with* (συμμαρτυρεῖ) *our soul that we are children* (τέκνα) *of God* (8 : 16). The Vulgate renders this verse incorrectly. *The Spirit bears witness to our spirit.* . . . The meaning of συμμαρτυρεῖν is *to join in bearing witness*, and on the only other two occasions the word is used by St. Paul (Ros. 2 : 15 ; 9 : 1) this is the exact meaning. The Greek word τέκνον "child" has a connotation that is not found in υἱός, also meaning "child", "son". The word υἱός can be applied to an adopted son, whereas τέκνον means a son in the ordinary process of nature. This contrast between the two concepts is illustrated by St. Paul. Every soul has an intimation that it is the handiwork of God, just as the article of furniture is the handiwork of the craftsman (τέκτων); whereas the Holy Spirit diffused in the soul through grace makes of each one a child (υἱός) of God (Ros. 8 : 15).

Hope of redemption

The hope of a Redeemer to come, given by God to Adam after his fall, was transmitted to every child of Adam, just as the consequences of Adam's sin were transmitted. Hope of redemption means hope of securing something that has been lost. The prisoner or slave has lost his liberty and is conscious of the loss. By Adam's sin all nature was condemned to slavery (Ros. 8 : 21), and all mankind became slaves of the devil (Ac. 26 : 18); and, according to St. Paul, every human soul is conscious of having lost the patrimony due to it as a child of God. Otherwise the hope of redemption would have no meaning. St. Paul also implies that throughout life every human soul is yearning to meet God to be restored to its lost privileges. Even irrational nature (κτῆσις), which also incurred slavery by Adam's sin, is animated with that hope of redemption, of recovering the divine glory that was lost. *The creation in ardent expectation eagerly awaits the revelation of the glory of the sons of God. For creation was subjected to frustration not through wilful fault, but through fault of him who subjected it; and is dependent on the hope that creation itself also will be released from the slavery of destruction unto the freedom of the glory of the children of God* (Ros. 8 : 19–21). That is, irrational creation reveals, by its instincts and impulses, that it is conscious of having lost the divine glory with which it was endowed, and in a state of utter tension is enduring the throes of parturition (8 : 22), as it were, in the hope of recovering its lost privileges. This analogy applies also to rational creation as a whole. Mankind universally, not any mere section, are represented as yearning for the privilege of sonship of God which they forfeited by Adam's sin, and anxiously awaiting the day when they will meet God to hear his verdict: *And not only [irrational] creation but ourselves also —even we ourselves who have the first fruits of the Spirit—we are groaning within ourselves for sonship, eagerly looking forward to release from our bodies* (8 : 23).

This verse 8 : 23 has been consistently mistranslated. *Not only creation but ourselves also. . . .* Who are represented by *ourselves also?* Commentators differ. Some say the apostles only. Others hold that the reference is to all Christians, including the apostles. The form of the sentence clearly indicates that *all mankind* are in question. The phrase ἀλλὰ καὶ αὐτοί *ourselves also* refers to the whole of rational creation. Then parenthetically it is stated that even Christians are included— *even we ourselves who have the first fruits of the Spirit* (τὴν ἀπαρχὴν τοῦ πνεύματος ἔχοντες ἡμεῖς καὶ αὐτοί). Just as irrational creation in its entirety (πᾶσα ἡ κτίσις, 8 : 22) is enduring the pangs of poignant expectancy awaiting its destiny, so too are all men yearning for their lost patrimony and longing for the day when the soul will be released from the body to meet God in judgement. This longing in creation, rational and irrational, is due to the hope of redemption which is present in each case. *For it is by hope we were saved* (Ros. 8 : 24).

St. Paul analyses the concept of hope to show why it is that the human soul is anxiously awaiting release from the body to secure its destiny. When our first parents were being expelled from Paradise God gave them and all their descendants hope of redemption, in the coming of the *seed of the woman* who would crush the serpent's head. *Hope which is seen*, says St. Paul, *is not hope, for who hopes for what he sees? But if we hope for what we do not see we eagerly await in a state of endurance* (24).

An analogy will help to an understanding of St. Paul's meaning here. Suppose a man sees a house and hopes that some day he will be its owner. He sees the house, but he does not yet see the ownership for which he hopes. That is still in the future—hope in the present, its realisation in the future. The two can never coexist. When the man becomes owner of the house, the hope of ownership is seen, that is realised. Then the hope itself disappears, *hope which is seen is not hope.* Similarly hope of redemption, of recovery of lost sonship, is throughout life present in every human soul; and can only be realised in the future, that is in the next life. Hence the soul's eager longing for release from the body (ἀπολύτρωσιν τοῦ σώματος, 23), to realise the hope of sonship through the promised Redeemer. While that hope is present in this life, and it is always present, it cannot be realised. Hope and its realisation cannot coexist.

St. Paul says that even we Christians, *who have the first fruits of the Spirit,* have retained this instinctive longing for sonship of God which was lost through Adam's sin. The human race was saved from the extinction of despair by the hope of a Redeemer, and this hope has through the thousands of years of waiting induced a *habitus* in the soul. Not even the assurance of the Holy Spirit that we are God's children, and heirs and coheirs of Christ, has removed from the soul this instinctive longing for the recovery of God's friendship. This attitude of the human soul is crystallised in the formula *anima humana naturaliter Christiana:* the human soul instinctively claiming union with Christ, the promised Redeemer.

A different interpretation

Commentators have taken an altogether different view of this passage (Ros. 8 : 23). They hold, as I have said, that St. Paul is speaking here only of Christians, whether apostles alone or others are included, and that the sonship for which the soul is longing is the resurrection or redemption of the body. There is no doubt whatever that in verse 23 all mankind are in question. Even if it were true that only Christians were mentioned, how can it be established that their ardent longing throughout life is for the resurrection of the body? St. Thomas Aquinas says the resurrection is the consummation of sonship. But this implies that even the blessed in Heaven, who are enjoying the Beatific Vision, are awaiting the resurrection in a state of tension and expectancy (25). Waiting for the resurrection entails no privation and therefore no suffering. The resurrection will surely come. Waiting for the divine privileges lost through Adam's delinquency is on quite a different footing. The resurrection will be of little avail to the soul that has not an assurance from God that it has been restored for eternity to his friendship. It is for this assurance the human soul is waiting in earnest and eager expectancy: When the soul meets God after release from the body will God acknowledge it as his child? This is the supreme moment for the soul.

When St. Paul was writing his Epistle to the Romans, Christians were only a tiny fraction of the human race. The vast multitude of men had never heard of the resurrection of the body, which is a purely revealed doctrine, and therefore could not hope for such an event. The hope of redemption is instinctively in the soul of every man. So also, according to St. Paul, is the eagerness to realise this hope by escaping from the prison of the body. It is not implied that the body is an evil thing. There is no suggestion of Manicheanism. But the body retards the homing instinct of the soul in its inborn anxiety to return to its Father, to be restored to its lost privileges.

Commentators who support the theory of the resurrection of the body in this passage are in difficulties to explain the sentence $\tau\hat{\eta}\ \gamma\grave{a}\rho\ \acute{\epsilon}\lambda\pi\iota\delta\iota\ \acute{\epsilon}\sigma\acute{\omega}\theta\eta\mu\epsilon\nu$. *For it is by hope we were saved* (8 : 24). Various versions, equally futile, have been suggested: "As far as hope is concerned we have been saved". Can we then dispense with hope and rely on faith and charity? "We have been saved for hope." "We have been saved after the manner of hope", that is we must still keep hoping! There is no question here of being saved in the sense of salvation being secured. St. Paul surely was no victim of such an illusion. *By hope we were saved* means that the hope of a Redeemer saved the human race from a despair which could result in its extinction. Man is conscious of having a soul created by God for a great destiny. If the hope of securing that destiny once vanished, man's *raison d'être* would also vanish. The word $\sigma\acute{\omega}\zeta\omega$ is frequently used of "saving life", and in the passive voice, as here, of "surviving". This hope of redemption is so native to the soul and so dominant in its influence that it has induced a *habitus*, which survives even in the christian soul, of looking forward with anxiety and endurance to its realisation (Ros. 8 : 25).

This passage (Ros. 8 : 18–26) is a digression stemming from the verse *heirs of God and coheirs of Christ, if, that is, we suffer with him in order to be glorified with him* (8 : 17). St. Paul proceeds to show that suffering in order to recover its destiny, lost by Adam's sin, is the lot of all creation, rational and irrational. The Christian who has the assurance of the Holy Spirit that he is the heir of God and coheir of Christ, if only he will suffer with Christ, should surely not grudge to endure the sufferings of this life which are trifling in comparison with the glory to come.

At verse 26 St. Paul returns to the subject of the Holy Spirit's operation in the soul, helping our weakness, and even when we know not what to pray for, interceding for us with *sighings without words*, for words are not necessary for the Searcher of hearts *who knows the meaning of the Spirit in the intercession he makes, in accordance with the divine will, for the holy ones of God.* (Ros. 8 : 26–27).

We have been examining the question of justification under the Natural Law. Without revelation man can, by observation and reason, discover the true God. His conscience which is his sole guide—*each one a law unto himself* (Ros. 2 : 14)—bids him worship God and obey God's commandments as *written in his heart*. His faith in the Redeemer promised to Adam unites him with Christ in the struggle against *the seed of the serpent. The lust of sin shall be under thee and thou shalt have dominion over it*, said God to Cain (Gen. 4 : 7). If he should fall into sin, forgiveness by God is inevitably at hand for the man united with the promised Redeemer by faith (Ros. 3 : 20–21).

In *Romans* vii St. Paul introduces a speaker who says *at one time outside the Law I lived*. The meaning of this statement, as we have seen[1], is that under the Natural Law this man enjoyed the grace and friendship of God, through his faith, of course, in the promised Redeemer; whereas under the abrogated Mosaic Law, which he adopted in good faith, he fell away from grace, and became the slave of sin, *sold away under sin;* because under the abrogated Mosaic Law he was completely cut adrift from Christ the Redeemer, the source of all grace (Gal. 5 : 3–4).

---

[1] ch. II., p. 27.

Jew versus gentile

St. Paul examines still further the prospect of salvation of the man living *bona fide* under the Natural Law as compared with that of the Jew under the abrogated Mosaic Law. The Jews despised the uncircumcised gentiles, regarding themselves as infinitely superior where God and religion were in question. They considered, in fact, that possession of the Law gave them a monopoly of the spiritual: *Thou claimest Jewish blood; thou reliest on the Law; God is all thy boast; thou canst tell what is his will, discern what things are of moment, because the Law has taught thee. Thou hast confidence in thyself as one who leads the blind, a light to their darkness; admonishing the fool, instructing the simple, because in the Law thou hast the incarnation of all knowledge and all truths* (Ros. 2 : 17–20). If Paul had taken to literature what entertaining satire he could have written! One also feels, in reading his letters, that if he had been pitted in the law courts against Demosthenes himself, the king of Attic oratory would not have emerged an easy victor. But we are discussing the gentile under the Natural Law as compared with the Jew under the abrogated Mosaic Law.

Jew and gentile are here contrasted by St. Paul not on the basis of the Mosaic Law, but of the Natural Law which was common to both,—the Natural Law being unwritten for the gentile, but written for the Jew and incorporated in the Mosaic Code. Paul warns that hearing a law read makes no difference. The Law was regularly read in the Synagogue. The gentiles had no law to read. *Doing* a law it is that counts before God (2 : 13). *You who forbid stealing do you steal? You who forbid adultery do you commit adultery? You who abominate idols do you rob the Temple?* (Ros. 2 : 21). These are commandments against the Natural Law. Jews were obliged by the Law to make contributions to the Temple, a duty which they often evaded by trickery such as supplying defective animals as victims (Matt. 1 : 7, 14). They thus by retaining what was due to the Temple, gave to the creature the honour due to the Creator, and as such were idol worshippers. Paul's argument is that the uncircumcised gentile who performs the commandments of the Natural Law though unwritten, will be justified on the day of judgement, ra ther than the circumcised Jew, who fails to carry out the commandments written though they are for him. *And uncircumcised though he is in nature's state, if he performs the law he will judge you who violate the law for all your circumcision and written word* (Ros. 2 : 17). The gentile who keeps the Natural Law will secure his salvation.

The vast majority of mankind in the period between Adam and Christ were dependent for their salvation on the Natural Law through the merits of the Redeemer promised to Adam. The Natural Law still obtains as the sole means of salvation for those whom the gospel message has not reached. While St. Paul leaves no doubt about the sufficiency of the Natural Law for those who are *bona fide* dependent on it, he implies by his scathing indictment of the gentiles' sins (Ros. 1 : 18–32) that the struggle of fallen human nature under the Natural Law was unequal. Idolatry was the besetting sin and the fertile source of moral degeneracy. *For the worship of abominable idols is the cause and beginning and end of all evil* (Wisd. 14 : 27).

Chapter Seven

JUSTIFICATION AND THE MOSAIC LAW

AFTER Adam's sin God promised the human race a Redeemer, a victory over the powers of evil through the *seed of the woman* (Gen. 3 : 15). This promise was made to mankind collectively. It is for each man with God's help and his own free will to ensure that he shares in the blessing promised to all.

This promise to the human race in general was followed by a special covenant with Noe (Gen. 9 : 1–17), which was followed by that with Abraham (Gen. 15–18 ; 17 : 7), succeeded in turn by that with Moses and the people of Israel. Noe was rescued from a mass of corruption to bring up a new people pleasing to God. Abraham was taken from the corrupt environment of Mesopotamia to the isolation of nomadic life in Canaan. Moses with his people was delivered from Egypt to enter as a nation into the land destined to be their home. These were the various landmarks in the history of the salvation of the human race through the promised Redeemer.

God's covenant with Noe promised the preservation of life henceforth after the destruction of the Deluge: *Whoever shall shed man's blood, his blood shall be shed; for man was made to the image of God* (Gen. 9 : 6). *And all flesh shall be no more destroyed with the waters of a flood* (11).

The covenant with Abraham

The covenant with Abraham was one of special significance. God promised Abraham the possession of the land of Canaan, the multiplication of his seed, the issue therefrom of kings (Gen. 17 : 6); *and promised him that in his seed all the nations of the earth should be blessed* (Gen. 12 : 3 ; 22 : 18). This was always recognised as a distinct promise of the Redeemer Christ. Abraham was the founder of the family from whom the chosen people had its origin. As a seal of this covenant, all the males of Abraham's household were to be circumcised (Gen. 17 : 11).

Strictly speaking the covenant with Abraham was a promise given by God in recognition of his wonderful faith. The promise was absolute. Abraham was admonished by God to lead a life of holiness in conformity with the divine will: *Walk before me and be perfect* (Gen. 17 : 1). All human feelings and considerations were to give way to the divine will. Abraham was destined to be the teacher and model for posterity unto distant generations. The promises made to Abraham were repeated by God to Isaac and Jacob. Through Abraham and his descendants, the patriarchs, the knowledge of the one true God should be transmitted and given to the entire world (Gen. 18 : 18).

The descendants of the patriarchs had become a people in Egypt. Here they were oppressed by Pharaoh and there was a danger that they would submit to their fate and lose consciousness of the promises made to their fathers. At this juncture God called Moses to lead the people out of Egypt into the land promised to the patriarchs. The mission of Moses was one of the most important events in the religious history of mankind. Israel, as the chosen people were known, being descended from the family of Jacob, had been God's people before the time of Moses. Now God decreed to initiate a more intimate relationship and make a special covenant with his people. Moses, Israel's leader, was to act as mediator in the ratification of this covenant. The religion of the patriarchs was based on a special revelation from God. The new covenant with his chosen people is a continuation and development of this revelation, covering all the relations of their future religious and social life as a nation. The Law, said to have been given to Moses by angels, was freely accepted by the people of Israel.

The Law of Moses

The purpose of the Law was not to undo or qualify in any way the promise made to Abraham some four hundred years previously. The covenant with Abraham was the basis of the new covenant with the people of Israel, and the purpose of this covenant was to bring to fulfilment the promise to Abraham that *in his seed all the nations of the earth should be blessed. The Law*, says St. Paul, *was also given (προσετέθη) because of transgressions, until the coming of the seed for whom the promise was made* (Gal. 3 : 18). The human race ever since Adam's fall was prone to idolatry, and idolatry in turn, has ever been the fruitful source of moral degradation (Ros. 1 : 24–26). Just as Abraham was called by God to leave his home and people and travel into a far distant strange land, in preparation for the role he was destined to play in the salvation of the human race, so by the Mosaic Law, Israel is made a people apart from other peoples in her way of living and thinking. "She is the seed of a new humanity, called to transform the whole of mankind."[1] *It is not for you to live by the customs of that Egyptian land in which you once dwelt, or to imitate the men of Canaan, and follow their observances. It is my decrees you will execute, my commands you will obey, . . . am I not the Lord your God* (Lev. 18 : 3–4). *It is not for you to imitate the practices of the nations I am driving out to make room for you. Was it not these very practices that made me their enemy?* (Lev. 20 : 23). The Law was given *because of transgressions*, to preserve this one people from the corruption of the surrounding nations.

Holiness of life was the primary consideration in the covenant of God with Israel. *If therefore you will hear my voice and keep my covenant, you shall be my peculiar possession above all people, and you shall be to me a priestly kingdom and a holy nation.* Israel freely accepted the covenant: *And all the people answered together, all the Lord hath spoken we will do* (Exod. 19 : 5–8). A curse was invoked upon him who failed to observe the Law: *Cursed be he who abideth not in the words of the Law and fulfils them not in works* (Deut. 27 : 26).

The covenant between God and Israel was not one of mere cold formality. *With unchanging love I love thee . . . Israel, poor homeless maid* (Jer. 31 : 3). "She is not simply one of the peoples of the earth: she is the beginning, the seed of a new man, of man in the image and likeness of God, called to have a part in his personal life. Israel is not simply a new kind of nation—rather a new kind of humanity appears in her: for Israel is the beginning of the making supernatural of mankind, that radical transformation

---

[1]Claude Tresmontant, *St. Paul and the Mystery of Christ*, p. 67.

which is to make man capable and worthy of divine adoption. Israel is already the Church, the Lord's bride, the mystical body of Christ."[1] The instrument chosen by God to mould Israel into *a royal priesthood and a consecrated nation* was the Law of Moses. The Law of Moses was to be her teacher, *her pedagogue to Christ* (Gal. 3 : 24). *For Christ was the end of the Law* (Ros. 10 : 4).

It was the Law of Moses "that distinguished Israel from all the other peoples, the Law, the totality of God's commandments, that kept her from the corruptions of her neighbours: it was both her backbone and her bulwark. Without the Law there could have been no Israel, because like other nations she would have gone after false Gods and befouled herself with wickedness and criminality."[2]

Monotheism

Monotheism, the worship of the one true God, was the foundation stone of the Old Testament religion; and this characteristic isolates and distinguishes it from every other religion of the ancient world. The fundamentals of the Mosaic Law are the basis of the New Dispensation, for the substance of both is the obligation of loving God and neighbour. Asked by a doctor of the Law what was the greatest commandment of the Law, Jesus replied: *You shall love the Lord your God with your whole heart. This is the greatest and the first commandment. The second is similar to it, you shall love your neighbour as yourself. On these two commandments depend the whole Law and the Prophets* (Matt. 22 : 36–40).

The Mosaic Law was not an end in itself. It was a pedagogue leading Israel to Christ, and through Israel all mankind. *Salvation is to come from the Jews* (Jn. 4 : 22). The Law was powerless of itself to sanctify or give grace, being but an instrument in the hands of sinful nature (Ros. 8 : 3). The Law acquired all its spiritual efficacy through its connexion with Christ for whom it was ordained in the first instance . . . *until the coming of the seed*. It was the instrument, as we have seen, chosen by God to sanctify his chosen people. *Keep my law and my judgements, which if a man do he shall live by them* (Lev. 18 : 5). When a doctor of the

---

[1] *Id. ibid.*, p. 65.

[2] *Id. ibid.*, p. 66.

Law asked Christ what should he do to win eternal life, Christ asked him *what is written in the law? How readest thou?* When the doctor replied, reading the commandment to love God and the neighbour, Christ said: *thou hast answered aright, this do and thou shalt live* (Lk. 10 : 26–28). It was on the Mosaic Law that Zachary and Elizabeth, Simeon and Anna, to mention but a few of the names familiar through the New Testament, depended for their sanctification. It was through the Mosaic Law that Christ sanctified his Apostles and disciples during his mission on earth. He was born and lived under the Law, and came to bring the Law to its issue and fulfilment. *Whoever then sets aside one of these commandments (of the Law) though it were the least . . . will be of little account in the kingdom of heaven; but the man who keeps them and teaches others to keep them will be accounted in the kingdom of heaven as the greatest* (Matt. 5 : 19). The people of Israel for a period of thirteen hundred years depended for their salvation on the Mosaic Law, violation of which called down a curse on the offender.

The Law was a pedagogue leading to Christ (Gal. 3 : 28). It was the duty of a pedagogue to take his master's children to and from school and assist them at their lessons. While Israel was a minor, needing milk rather than solid food (Hebr. 5 : 12 ff.) this was also the function of the Law; but when Israel reached its majority, the function of the Law ceased to exist. *For Christ is the end of the Law bringing justification to everyone who believes in him* (Ros. 10 : 4). By his death on the cross the old order was terminated, the Law was fulfilled and abrogated and the New Dispensation instituted. *Men do not put new wine into old bottles* (Mark 9 : 17). On the night before his death Jesus established the Covenant proclaimed by the prophets, ratified not through the blood of animals as Moses ratified the Covenant on Mount Sinai, but through his own blood on Calvary.

On the first Pentecost some three thousand converts responded to the preaching of the Apostles . . . *You shall be witnesses to me in Jerusalem and in all Judea and even to the utmost parts of the earth* (Ac. 1 : 8). *He that believes and is baptised shall be saved* (Mk. 16 : 16). Baptism is the condition of membership of Christ's kingdom on earth. But for Jews, circumcision was a sacred rite of long standing and they found it difficult to believe that it was possible for the uncircumcised to be considered worthy of God's recognition. Christ himself had been circumcised and surely his followers must submit to that sacred rite. The early converts in Jerusalem were Jews for the most part and they continued to observe the Mosaic Law in the New Dispensation. Gentiles who were admitted in the early years were compelled to submit to the rite of circumcision. It was only after some ten years that the visions and other signs attending the conversion of Cornelius intimated to Peter and through him to the Mother Church of Jerusalem, that gentiles might be received without circumcision. The conversion of Cornelius was an epoch-making event, and St. Luke recognised it as such, recording it like the conversion of St. Paul, another epoch-making event, three times in the *Acts of the Apostles*.

The conversion of Cornelius

There was at Caesarea a centurion named Cornelius . . . a pious man who worshipped the true God, like all his household, gave alms freely . . . and prayed to God continually (Acts 10 : 1–2). Cornelius was a non-commissioned officer of the Roman army. "Fearing God" was the usual term for uncircumcised proselytes who accepted the Jewish faith and often many of its practices. About three o'clock one afternoon Cornelius had a vision in which he clearly saw an angel of God come into his home and address him by name. *What is it, Lord?* he asked gazing in terror at his visitor. The angel replied, *thy prayers and alms deeds are recorded on high in God's sight. And now he would have you send men to Joppa, to bring here one Simon, surnamed Peter. . . . You will learn from him what you must do* (Ac. 10 : 5–7).

The angel departed. Cornelius summoned two of his servants and a soldier, a man of piety, told them what had happened and despatched them to Joppa. The scene now is changed to Joppa. Peter, we are told by St. Luke, had gone up to the housetop about noon to pray, as Jews were wont to do. He was hungry and waiting for a meal, and while the meal was in preparation St. Peter fell into an ecstasy. He saw heaven open and a bundle, like a great sheet, let down by its four corners on to the earth. In it were all kinds of fourfooted beasts and things that creep on the earth and all the birds of the air. And a voice came to him, *Rise up, Peter, kill and eat.* Peter answered, *by no means, Lord. Never in my life have I eaten anything profane and unclean.* Then the voice came a second time, *It is not for you to call anything profane which God has made clean.* This happened, we are told, three times and then the bundle was drawn back into heaven.

St. Luke continues: Peter was still puzzling in his mind over the meaning of the vision when the messengers from Cornelius were seen standing at the gate. They inquired for Simon called Peter. *To Peter, as he was turning over the vision in his mind, the Spirit said, here are three men asking for you; rise and go down and accompany them without misgiving. It is I who have sent them* (Ac. 10 : 19–20). Peter went down and inquired for the visitors' business. They replied that they had come from Cornelius . . . who had received a revelation from one of the holy angels that *he was to bring you to his home and listen to what you would say.* Next day Peter set out with the visitors, accompanied by some local Christians.

The following day they reached Caesarea, where they found Cornelius expecting them, surrounded by kinsmen and intimate friends, *a great company*, as St. Luke describes them. St. Peter now speaks: *You know well enough that a Jew is contaminated if he consorts with one of another race or visits him. But God has been showing me that we ought not to speak of any man as unclean; and so when I was sent for I came without demur. Tell me then, why have you sent for me?* All this is told in St. Luke's limpid Greek. Cornelius told his story, thanked Peter and said, *Now you see us assembled here in your presence, ready to listen to whatever charge the Lord has given you.* Thereupon St. Peter gave a brief instruction, outlining the history of salvation through Christ : *All the prophets bear him this testimony that everyone who has faith in him finds forgiveness of sin in his name* (Ac. 10:43). The following is the important point: *Before Peter had finished speaking to them there, the Holy Spirit fell on all those who were listening to his message, for they began speaking with tongues and proclaiming the greatness of God* (Ac. 10 : 44, 46). That is, before they were baptised, the Holy Spirit descended on these gentiles, with miraculous signs such as occurred on the first Pentecost. This is the only recorded case of the reception of the Holy Spirit before Baptism. The purpose of this miraculous intervention was to intimate to the Apostle Peter God's will, that gentiles were to be henceforth admitted to the Church without the conditions of circumcision and acceptance of the Mosaic Law.

Baptism without circumcision

Once gentiles were admitted to the Church without circumcision, the breach with the Synagogue becomes formal. The Church can no longer be considered a Jewish sect. Christianity becomes an independent religion. Thus it was miraculously reserved to St. Peter to make the greatest decision the Apostles ever made, and subsequently to hold the Church to this decision in the teeth of strong opposition. It was necessary to reaffirm this decision at the Council of Jerusalem some ten years afterwards.

St. Paul now enters the scene. Antioch was the third city of the Roman Empire, ranking after Rome and Alexandria. It had over one million inhabitants. The city was famous for its Hellenic culture and philosophers, for its monuments and for its licentiousness. Here the gospel was preached and gentiles were admitted to the Church on the same terms as in the case of Cornelius, without circumcision. Word of this reached the Mother Church at Jerusalem and the authorities there sent Barnabas on a mission of inquiry to Antioch. Himself a Hellenist from Cyprus and enjoying the confidence of the Apostles, the warmhearted Barnabas was the ideal man for the occasion. Barnabas was delighted with what met his eyes in Antioch, the evidence of the Holy Spirit in the changed lives of these pagan converts. Evidently the Jewish element in Antioch resented the bypassing of circumcision in the process of conversion and sneered at the new sect, the *Christians* who chose Christ as their leader, and presumed to ignore the Mosaic Law. The nickname given in derision stuck, however, like that of Jesuit and others in later times. Barnabas, the official emissary from Jerusalem, encouraged the *Christians* and now summoned to his aid a fellow-Hellenist named Paul of Tarsus. For about a year Paul worked under the supervision of Barnabas, an eventful year in the course of which the Church of Antioch developed a missionary zeal that gave it a position of importance prior even to that of the Mother Church in Jerusalem. St. Peter's decision in the case of Cornelius was at the root of this development.

The Council of Jerusalem

Some three or four years passed during which Paul and Barnabas had been zealously preaching the gospel throughout the East, preaching salvation through faith in Christ and ignoring the claims of the Mosaic Law. And again they were back in Antioch in the Autumn of 49. The Church in Jerusalem, even though it had accepted the decision in the case of Cornelius (Ac. 11 : 18), was still hankering after the Temple and the Law. Now a party, led by believing Pharisees, had gone down to Antioch and began to tell the brethren there, *You cannot be saved without being circumcised according to the tradition of Moses* (Ac. 15 : 1). Here was a direct challenge to Paul and Barnabas. The validity of their conversions during their missionary labours, so vividly outlined in *Acts* xiii and xiv, was now publicly questioned. Must the Mosaic Law be enforced after all? Must every Christian be circumcised? It was decided that Paul and Barnabas and *certain of the rest* should go up to see the Apostles and presbyters in Jerusalem about the question (15 : 2). This assembly was called the Council of Jerusalem.

St. Peter again clinched the issue. Addressing the Judaizers, as the champions of Judaism were called, he said: *How is it that you would now call God in question by putting a yoke on the necks of the disciples such as we and our fathers have been too weak to bear?* (Ac. 15 : 10). The Council's decision was: *It has seemed good to the Holy Spirit and to us that no burden should be laid upon you beyond those which cannot be avoided* (Ac. 15 : 28).

The question at issue in the Council of Jerusalem was one of supreme moment in view of Christ's command to teach all nations. Was the institution for continuing Christ's mission of salvation to be Jewish and national, a mere outgrowth of the Synagogue, or Christian and universal? Was circumcision, a rite so objectionable to gentiles, to be obligatory on all? Was the Mosaic Law with all its precepts, all its taboos in the matter of food and ablutions and associations, to be imposed on all mankind? Judaism, of its very nature, was an exclusive religion, designed by God as such, to protect his chosen people from the contamination of the nations. It had already proved the great barrier against the levelling force of Hellenism. Judaism and Catholicism were contradictory terms.

The Mosaic Law, set aside by the death of Christ, was now formally abrogated through the guidance of the Holy Spirit. The break with the Synagogue, however, was not immediate. In the beginning concessions were made to Jewish susceptibilities. Christians of Jewish origin might follow the Law, fulfilling it "in the light of Christ". But it was found that compromise in this delicate situation easily led to misunderstanding. What one man took to be supererogation would be considered by his neighbour as obligation. Ultimately all participation in Jewish rites was forbidden to Christians as unlawful.

The Epistle to the Galatians

Judaism, however, did not yield without a struggle. The false brethren who had challenged Paul's vindication of liberty in Christ for his disciples in Antioch, and had failed in the effort, now passed over to Galatia where they met with more success, although Jews were in a minority among the Galatian Christians. This was the occasion that called forth the Epistle to the Galatians. Here St. Paul ruthlessly exposes the futility of the abrogated Law, as a means of salvation. Not only is the Law worthless in itself, it is an immediate occasion of sin for those who rely on it, for they are bound by all the precepts of the Law, and being cut away from grace they cannot fulfil a single precept. This is the grave admonition St. Paul gives, issued with all the authority of an Apostle: *Lo, I Paul, tell you that if you become circumcised, Christ will avail you naught. Again I bear witness to everyman who is circumcised that he is bound to carry out the whole Law. In seeking for justification through the Law you have been cut adrift from Christ, you have fallen away from grace* (Gal. 5 : 2-4). Language could not be plainer. If the precepts of the Law be binding and precepts cannot be observed without grace, then without any doubt *through the Law comes knowledge of sin* (Ros. 3 : 20).

Opinions of commentators

All commentators must admit that St. Paul's condemnation of the Law as a means of salvation in *Galatians* 5 : 2-4, refers and can refer only, to the abrogated Law. But commentators generally, erroneously apply St. Paul's strictures on the abrogated Law to the divinely instituted Law which was in force from the days of Moses until the death of Christ. *The Mosaic Law*, we are told, *was the auxiliary of sin, it augmented prevarications and enkindled the divine wrath.* The Mosaic Law was introduced, in the first instance, *to make room for transgressions . . . that is to turn our sins into transgressions, make us conscious of them as a breach of a divine law and therefore of our need for redemption.* The divinely instituted Mosaic Law, we are told, *brought knowledge of sin, but not its remission. It was designed to make men conscious of their own sinfulness and so to make them long for the promised Redeemer.* . . . *The Mosaic Law imposed obligations, but gave no grace to perform the obligations and could not be observed.* . . . The expression of St. Paul: *The Law entered in that sin might abound* (Ros. 5 : 20) is taken to refer to the giving of the Law to Moses in the first instance. *Many commentators,* it is said, *find a definite design of God in the giving of the Law, not in the sense that God aimed at the increase of sin, but in the sense that the increase of sin would drive sinners to look for pardon.* . . . *The challenge to concupiscence of the huge corpus of positive law in the Mosaic system was too strong; and lacking the grace helps of Christianity the Jews became formal and conscious sinners.* . . . *Sin was permitted to use a holy and venerable thing* (*the Mosaic Law*) *for its own purposes, that men might realise its power and perversity—that it might appear in its true colours; and that men dreading its power and conscious of their own weakness might humbly seek help and deliverance from God.* . . . *It was God's gracious plan to bring home to men by the Law the sense of their own proneness to sin and their need of God's grace.* . . . *The really anomalous position is that of the Jewish world, subject to a Law which exposes and condemns sin, but offers no means of avoiding either it or its consequences.* . . . *The Law pointed out sin but gave no grace to avoid it.*

These opinions, taken from the works of various commentators, insist that the divinely instituted Mosaic Law imposed obligations but gave no grace to perform these obligations, and could not be observed; any attempt to observe the Law issued in sin. We are told that it was "God's gracious plan" to bring home to men by means of the Law the sense of their own proneness to sin and their need of God's grace.

We have seen that the purpose of the Mosaic Law, given to his beloved people by God, was *to make of them his peculiar possession above all people, a priestly kingdom and a holy nation.* The Law called down a curse on him who failed to fulfil its precepts. The Law was a pedagogue leading Israel to Christ, but, according to the commentators, the pedagogue had no option but to lead Israel along the way of sin, in order to make of them a holy nation. We have seen what Christ himself said: *Whoever sets aside one of these commandments (of the Law) though it were the least . . . will be of least account in the kingdom of heaven; but the man who keeps them and teaches others to keep them will be accounted in the kingdom of heaven as the greatest* (Matt. 5 : 19). The commentators tell us that these commandments of the Mosaic Law could not be kept.

The commentators rely for this extraordinary theory of the Mosaic Law on certain passages from the Epistles of St. Paul, especially the Epistle to the Romans, and particularly on chapter 7, 7–25 of the epistle. These passages have been completely misinterpreted. There is not a scintilla of evidence in St. Paul's epistles, or anywhere in Scripture as far as I know, for this view of the Mosaic Law. Everything that commentators have said about the Mosaic Law, during the period of its regime, applies exactly to the Law when it ceased to be a Law, when nothing remained but the letter of the Law, when it was automatically set aside by the death of Christ and formally abrogated by the Council of Jerusalem, some ten or fifteen years afterwards. Thenceforth, according to St. Paul, the Law was binding on those who persisted in following it as a way of salvation. Thenceforth every commandment of the abrogated Law that called for fulfilment could not be fulfilled and issued in sin, issued in *a harvest of death*. St. Paul solemnly proclaimed this doctrine in *Galatians* 5 : 2–5, the passage which I have quoted. He proves this doctrine in *Romans* 7 : 7–25, by giving the practical case of a man, who is introduced by St. Paul as an objector, and who had in good faith adopted the abrogated Law as a way of salvation. This objector, a mouthpiece for St. Paul's views, reveals his own spiritual condition before he adopted the Law and afterwards. The vast majority of the Jews still adhered to the abrogated Law as being in itself sufficient for salvation. "False brethren," the Judaizers tried to impose the abrogated Law on Christian converts, as being equally essential with baptism.

Some few commentators think that in this much discussed passage *Romans* 7 : 7–25, St. Paul is revealing his own spiritual difficulties as a Christian, and the difficulties of Christians in general in their struggle with the flesh. We shall deal with this view later. The majority of commentators hold that the speaker or objector in the passage, who introduces himself in the first person in verse 7, is an Israelite *under the regime of the Mosaic Law*, that he reveals the sinfulness and impossibility of the Law, ultimately crying out in anguish *who will release me from this body of death?*

The following is the passage in question, *Romans* 7 : 7–25. I shall begin with verse 5:

> 5. *For when we were in the power of the flesh the sinful passions aroused by the Law worked in our members to bear a harvest for death.* 6. *But now we have been released from the Law, having died to that whereby we were held captive, so that we are slaves of the spirit in the new life, not of the letter as of old.* 7. *What then shall we say? Is the Law sin? May it not prove so! But sin I knew not except through the Law, for desire I knew not (as sin) if the Law did not state "thou shalt not desire".* 8. *But sin taking its starting point through the Law wrought in me every form of desire, for apart from the Law sin was dead.* 9. *At one time outside the Law I lived. But when the commandment came, sin revived, and I died.* 10. *And the commandment that was intended for life turned out in my case to be one for death.* 11. *For sin taking its starting point through the commandment, deceived me and through it, killed me.* 12. *And yet the Law is holy, and the commandment is holy and just and good.* 13. *Has the good thing become death for me? God forbid! But it is sin that has proved death, operating through the good thing, to prove its sinfulness, so that sin, operating through the commandment, may prove sinful in the extreme.* 14. *For we know that the Law is spiritual, but I am of the flesh sold in slavery under the power of sin.* 15. *I understand not my actions. For it is not what I wish to do that I do, but what I hate, I do.* 16. *But even though I do what I do not wish to do, I agree that the Law is holy.* 17. *But as it is, it is not I who do the thing but the sin that dwells within me.* 18. *For I know that there does not dwell within me, that is in my flesh, anything good. For the will to do is there, but the accomplishing of the good is not there.* 19. *For I do not the good I wish but the evil I do not wish, that I do.* 20. *But if I do that which I do*

*not wish, then it is not I who do it, but the sinfulness that
dwells within me. 21. I find the principle operating that
while I wish to do what is good, it is the evil that is at hand
for me. 22. For according to the inner man I rejoice in the
Law of God. 23. But I see another law in my members
at war with the law of my mind and holding me a prisoner
to the law of sin that is in my members. 24. Unhappy man!
Who will rescue me from this body of death? 25. Thanks be
to God through Jesus Christ our Lord. Left to myself then,
in my mind I am slave to the Law of God, but in my flesh
to the law of sin.*

One distinguished commentator, the late Père Prat says that
the whole context of this extract cries out from the first line to
the last that the Speaker—the *I* of *I knew sin only through the
Law* (v. 7)—represents mankind in the grip of concupiscence
under the regime of the Law, and too feeble to prevail in this
unequal contest. Such, he says, was the unanimous opinion of
the Fathers before St. Augustine and such is the general opinion
of exegetes in modern times. This interpretation alone, Père Prat
continues, can explain many expressions in this passage. . . .
The Apostle, according to this commentator, wanted to prove
that the Mosaic Law deserved to perish as being the auxiliary of
sin and as provoking God's wrath in multiplying transgressions.
Père Prat quotes six texts from the Epistles of St. Paul (all except
one from *Romans*), which he says, *condemn the Law:*[1] *Romans* 4 : 13;
5 : 20; 3 : 20; 4 : 15; 7 : 8; 1 *Cor.* 15 : 56. According to Père Prat
the Law, the Mosaic Law in regime, was defective and had to be
set aside as such. Père Lagrange[2] does not admit that the Law was
itself defective. The deficiency lay with sinful men. But he also
agrees generally with the views of Père Prat on the Mosaic Law
during its period of regime. All the commentators whose work
I have seen, hold these same views. It may seem rash to question
what is apparently the unanimous opinion of distinguished
scholars, but the evidence in its entirety is there for all to see.
Let us examine it, beginning with *Romans* VII.

---

[1] *La Theologie de St. Paul*, Pt. 1 (tenth edit.), p. 275. For his view see
pp. 214–218; 267–278.

[2] Saint Paul *Epitre aux Romains*, p. 166.

Romans 7 : 7–25.

As I have said already, no commentator will question it that
the Law against which St. Paul is solemnly warning his Galatian
friends, in *Galatians* 5 : 2–4, is the abrogated Mosaic Law: *If
you become circumcised Christ will be of no avail to you. I bear
witness again to every man that is circumcised that he is bound to
observe the Law in its entirety. In seeking your justification through
the Law you have been cut adrift from Christ, you have fallen away
from grace.* This was the spiritual condition of Paul himself and
of his Jewish convert friends before they were baptised. In the
opening verses of chapter vii St. Paul reminds his friends that
just as marriage is dissolved by the death of the husband, so
also union with the Law is dissolved by the mystic death of
baptism, symbolised by immersion. The new life effected by
baptism means union with the risen Christ, issuing in a harvest of
good work for God. It means service of the spirit, whereas
formerly they were prisoners of *the letter of the Law* (7 : 6), and
slaves of the flesh, with the result that *the sinful passions aroused
by the Law operated in our members to produce a harvest for death*
(7 : 5). It is this statement of St. Paul, *the sinful passions aroused
by the Law,* (7 : 5) that calls for explanation. Is he suggesting that
the life of the Jews before their conversion, the life of the vast
majority of the Jewish people at the time St. Paul was writing,
was a life of sin, *a harvest for death*? The Law under which
St. Paul lived before his conversion was the Law abrogated by
the death of Christ. Note here how St. Paul identifies himself
with his correspondents, *when we were in the power of the flesh
. . . in our members . . . now we have been released from the Law
in which we were held captive.* The Law about which St. Paul
is speaking is beyond doubt the Law under which he and his
friends lived before their conversion. If St. Paul meant to speak
here of the Mosaic Law which was in force some thirty years
previously, surely he should have said so. Nothing now remains
but the letter of that Law (7 : 6); and the sinful passions which
it arouses, because it cannot be fulfilled, produce a harvest for
death.

The question naturally arises *Is the Law sin?* Without committing himself, St. Paul replies *may it not prove so!* (μή γένοιτο)
sometimes translated *God forbid!* At this stage (v. 7) a new speaker

intervenes to prove that in his case the Law has turned out to be sin. This is the rhetorical figure called the Diatribe, common in the philosophical discussions of the time. The figure gives the discourse a quality of objectivity and dramatic vitality. A new speaker is introduced. In the Platonic dialogues a different speaker is introduced to play each part, like an actor on the stage. In the Diatribe we can judge only from the context that a new speaker has been introduced. Who is the Speaker who has been introduced here (7 : 7), and what is his message?

Before dealing with these questions there are a few technical terms that call for explanation. What is the meaning of the expressions *to be in the flesh*, or *to be slave of the flesh?*, *to be slave of the spirit?*, *the sinful passions aroused by the Law?* When St. Paul describes himself and his friends as being formerly *in the power of the flesh*, he means that they were in the state of fallen naturel shut out from grace, just the spiritual condition of Adam after his sin, and before he got the promise of a Redeemer. He had lost all the supernatural gifts in which he had been created. The soul in this condition is in a state of spiritual death, at enmity with God and can do nothing to please God (Ros. 8 : 6–7), because it is cut off from grace. The actions of such a soul are on the purely natural level. No matter how well disposed he is, man cannot discharge his obligations to God without the aid of grace. *Not that we are sufficient of ourselves to think anything as from ourselves* (2 Cor. 3 : 5). Grace is the principle that supernaturalises actions. And Christ is the sole source of grace. *Without me you can do nothing* (Jn. 15 : 5). The soul that is cut off from contact with Christ is dependent on unaided sinful human nature (*the flesh*) and can discharge no obligation to God. No matter how ethically the good pagan lives, his life without grace is out of harmony with the divine will. When a man is *dependent on the spirit* he is guided by the promptings of the soul illumined by grace. In our examination of the passage 7 : 7–25 we shall see illustrated the meaning of the phrase, *the sinful passions aroused by the Law.*

Who is the Speaker?

When St. Paul says in answer to the question *Is the Law sin?* *God forbid* or more literally and correctly, *may it not prove so*, then the new Speaker says: *Well, it was only through the Law I knew sin . . . one time outside the Law I lived*. This is the only glimpse of the Speaker's personal history given us. Outside the Law at one time he lived. Now, beyond all doubt the word *I lived* (ἔζων) means *I lived the life of grace* in God's friendship. In the next breath he tells us he died (ἀπέθανον) when he was faced with the commandment of the Law. That means that he fell from the life of grace. The Speaker then, at one period of his history, was outside the realm of the Mosaic Law. What can that mean except that at one time he was a gentile living under the Natural Law? We shall see that he knows nothing about Christ or Christianity. There were only two great divisions of mankind, Jew and gentile. He was a gentile. He is now a Jew. He has embraced the Mosaic Law, hoping to find therein his salvation.

Commentators who hold that the Speaker is a young Israelite speaking not exclusively for himself but for Israelites living under the Law during the period of its regime,—and this is the view of the vast majority—must solve a difficulty. St. Paul, they hold, is himself adopting this role, giving his views as a young Israelite through the mouth of the Speaker. At what period in his life was St. Paul or any other Israelite *outside the Law?* Commentators say that the clause *one time outside the Law I lived* covers the period of Paul's childhood up to the use of reason, when knowledge of the Law, they maintain, brought sin for the first time. The Mosaic Law prescribed circumcision for every male child on the eighth day after his birth. This precept of the Law, we know, was fulfilled in St. Paul's case (Phil. 3 : 5). If, during his period of childhood, young Paul was in the state of grace (*I lived*), it was due to circumcision, one of the first precepts of the Law, which according to theologians remitted original sin. The only time that Paul or any other young Israelite could be said to be *outside the Law*, was during the first seven days of his childhood, before circumcision.

The Speaker then was not a native born Israelite. At one period he was a gentile—*outside the Law* has no other meaning. He tells us that as a gentile he lived a life of grace. Note the imperfect *I used to live* (ἔζων). At some period of his life he adopted the Mosaic Law, evidently in good faith, thinking that it was the Law of God. He was a holy, conscientious man. We can take it that he was circumcised. He was wholly dedicated to the Mosaic Law, *in my mind a slave of the Law* (7 : 25). He was convinced that *the Law was holy and the commandment holy and just and good* (12). He relates his spiritual experience under the Law. He broke the commandment *thou shalt not covet*. Concupiscence in connexion with this sin, had been dead in his case, for the Natural Law, under which he had previously lived, did not take cognisance of mere thoughts or desires. Note how he uses the imperfect again, *for desire I used not to recognise* but the aorist, *sin I did not commit except through the Law*. Under the Natural Law then, the Speaker lived a life of grace. He did not regard thoughts or desires as sinful, and the concupiscence of that sin was dead in his case. Let it be noted here that the concupiscence to which he refers (v. 8) is definitely that of desire. This phrase has been incorrectly rendered, *apart from the Law sin* (*in general*) *is dead*. The context clearly shows that the Speaker refers to one particular kind of sin or concupiscence. Then, when he adopted the Mosaic Law, he was faced by the commandment *thou shalt not desire*, and in presence of the commandment, concupiscence came to life and he sinned mortally. The concupiscence of desire, taking advantage of the commandment, revived and being assailed with desires of every kind, he died (11). The concupiscence of desire *deceived* him. *The serpent deceived me*, said Eve (Gen. 3 : 13). The Speaker, just as Eve, had previously been in God's friendship and, like Eve, he was taken unawares by something completely new to him. But he does not deny his guilt, nor does he blame the Law or the commandments, for all his faith is in the Law. He can be described as a text-book case of the man who put his trust in the Law. *The Law is holy*, he says, and the commandment he violated is *holy and good and just*. He blames his own sinful concupiscence which used the holy commandment and wrought death in him. He asks himself could it be the commandment of the Law, the good thing, that proved deadly. God forbid! (13). For the Law is spiritual (14). The function of the Law was to bring life to the soul, not death. The Law was the instrument given by God to make a *holy people*, *a priestly nation*.

Sold away under sin

Now this holy man has fallen into sin and forfeited God's friendship; but with the excellent disposition he has, he should be able to recover God's friendship. He remains, however, in the power of the flesh. He has no contact with grace, no more than Adam had after his fall and before he was promised a Redeemer. He tells us *he is sold away under sin* (15) like a slave sold to a master, and that altogether against his will. He is in a quandary. He wills to do one thing, the good thing, that is, to please God; but he does the evil thing that he hates (15, 19). He admits he is powerless to escape from his position. He no longer blames himself. *It is not I who act thus, but the concupiscence that dwells within me* (17). *If I do not that which I wish, the action is no longer mine, but that of the concupiscence that dwells within me* (20). Note especially this: *The principle I find governing me is that whereas I will to do the good thing it is the evil thing that results* (21). The good or honourable thing is to keep God's law that he prizes so highly. His intellect and will are altogether on the side of the Law, *for according to the inner man my delight is in the Law of God*. But his intellect and will are of no avail. He remains a prisoner to the law of his members, which defies the law of his mind (22–23). He is completely at the mercy of his own sinful concupiscence, and ultimately he cries out in anguish *who will release me from this body of death?* (24). We shall see from what quarter release comes.

Père Prat says that the spiritual condition of the Speaker in this passage is that of a young Israelite under the Mosaic Law *during the regime of the Law*. Was it not possible then, under the Law, for a sinner who lost God's grace to recover it? Did he remain a prisoner *sold away under sin*? The case of David immediately occurs to the mind. David lived under the regime of the Law, and his sin was more deliberate and more heinous than the sin of the Speaker. Yet immediately that David confessed his sin, the prophet Nathan told him that his sin had been forgiven (2 Kgs. 12 : 13). Why is the Speaker's sin not forgiven? Why can he do nothing good, acceptable in God's sight, although he recognises the excellence of the Law and wholeheartedly wills to fulfil its precepts? The spiritual condition of the Israelites under the Mosaic Law was immeasurably more privileged than that of their gentile neighbours who lived under the Natural Law. Let us see how a gentile, who fell into sin, would have fared.

We are told in Genesis (3 : 15) that God promised Adam and his descendants a Redeemer, *the seed of the woman* who would be at enmity with the *seed of the serpent* and crush the serpent's head. God illustrated that revelation further to Cain, Adam's eldest son, who was meditating the murder of his brother Abel. *If thou do well, shalt thou not receive? but if ill shall not sin forthwith be at thy door? But the lust thereof shall be under thee, and thou shalt have dominion over it* (Gen. 4 : 7). What does this direct revelation of God mean? If a man does ill his sin is *at the door*. But God gives the immediate assurance that the sinner is not sold *away under sin*, the slave of sin, unless of course the sinner himself wills it. God assures Cain that he has authority and dominion over the lust of sin. Contrast this position with that of the Speaker in *Romans* VII. The lust of sin has him completely under its authority and dominion. Why the difference?

According to Père Prat the incident portrayed in the dramatic episode of *Romans* 7 : 7–25, could have occurred anytime in Israel during the regime of the Law, that is between the days of Moses and the death of Christ. The Speaker, he says, represents man in handigrips with concupiscence, *the lust of sin*, during the regime of the Law, and too feeble to obtain victory in the unequal struggle. And St. Paul's purpose, he says, in introducing this dramatic episode, is to show *that the Mosaic Law must go because it has been the auxiliary of sin and provoked the divine wrath by multiplying transgressions.*[1] In other words the Law could not be kept and every attempt to keep the Law issued in sin.

Let us suppose that the incident portrayed in *Romans* VII, occurred during the days of Moses and that Moses himself was listening to this young Israelite's account of his spiritual experience and heard his anguished appeal for help, *Who will deliver me from this body of death?* What would Moses have said? And the Lord spoke to Moses saying—Moses being the representative of God's chosen people—*You shall do my judgements and shall observe my precepts and shall walk in them, I am the Lord your God. . . . Keep my laws and my judgements, which if a man do he shall live by them. I am the Lord* (Lev. 8 : 1–5).

Let us suppose that the incident of this dramatic episode in *Romans*, occurred at the other end of the period covered by the regime of the Law, during Christ's public life; and that Christ himself heard the piteous cry for help of this young Israelite, as Père Prat describes him, what would Christ have said? We know exactly what Christ did say when a doctor of the Law asked him

[1] *op. cit.* p. 274.

what should he do to win eternal life. Christ said, *what is written in the Law? How readest thou?* The doctor read out the commandment to love God and the neighbour. Christ said *thou hast answered aright. This do and thou shalt live* (Lk. 10 : 26-28). Note the bearing of the doctor's question ... to win *eternal life,* and Christ's reply ... *thou shalt live;* and the statement in *Leviticus, he shall live by them* (18 : 5). *Eternal life* is the goal, not mere *length of days,* as some commentators on *Leviticus* hold. We know also what Christ said about violating the least of the commandments of the Law (Mt. 5 : 19). Very frequently, too, we meet in the Gospel that command of Christ when he has forgiven the sinner, *Go and sin no more.* For an Israelite living under the regime of the Law as Christ lived, *sin no more* means *keep the precepts of the Law.* The commentators tell us that the Law could not be kept. The Law, they say, pointed out sin but gave no grace to avoid it. Literally, *the Law entered in that sin might abound* (Ros. 5 : 20). The direct authority of St. Paul is quoted for this extraordinary theory of the Law. What is wrong?

The abrogated Law

Moses and Christ are speaking about one Law, the Law of Moses as it is called, instituted by God to sanctify Israel against the coming of the promised Redeemer, the *seed of the woman.* The episode in *Romans* 7 : 7-25 deals with another Law, rather the letter of the Law, the Law of Moses abrogated by the death of Christ and formally set aside by the Council of Jerusalem. Writing in 49 A.D.—whether immediately before or immediately after the Council of Jerusalem makes no difference—St. Paul solemnly warns the Galatians, *Lo, I Paul, tell you that if you become circumcised Christ will be of no avail to you. Again I bear witness to every man who is circumcised that he is under obligation to observe the whole Law. You whosoever seek justification through the Law have fallen away from grace* (Gal. 5 : 2-4). Paul himself had been circumcised. His warning is to those who are being circumcised now, and his warning includes all who seek justification through the Law, no matter when they were circumcised. This, of course, includes all who rejected justification through Christ, and sought to establish a justification of their own (Ros. 10 : 3), all who persist in following the abrogated Law. Commentators have confused these two periods of the Law. They have applied to the divinely instituted Law during its regime, the strictures of St. Paul on the abrogated Law. The Law, when set aside by the death of Christ, became the antagonist of Christ, entered into the list against Christ, and became, as St. Paul says, a *power for sin.*

In *Romans* VII St. Paul illustrates by a concrete example his teaching of *Galatians* 5 : 2–4. The Speaker introduced reveals his spiritual state, giving a true picture of his life before he embraced the Law and afterwards, the Law in question being the Mosaic Law as it existed at the time St. Paul was writing. If St. Paul were referring to the Law as it existed twenty or thirty years previously he surely would be bound to say so. Besides, the picture drawn here cannot represent the Law as it existed before the Christian era.

The Speaker tells us that he was a gentile at one period living in God's grace; that he ignored at that time the concupiscence of desire. There are theologians who claim that desire is forbidden by the Natural Law. St. Paul tells us that under the Natural Law each man is a law unto himself, having the precepts of the Law written in his heart. We must accept it then, that the Speaker is truly revealing the state of his conscience. *It is not the hearers of a law who are just in God's sight, but the doers of a law who will be justified . . . on the day God will judge the secret lives of men* (Ros. 2 : 13–16). Those living under the Natural Law had no written law to hear. The Jews, on the other hand, heard their Law being read out on certain occasions. St. Paul is contrasting, on the basis of the Natural Law which bound each party, the opportunities of salvation of the gentile under the Natural Law and the Jew under the abrogated Law. *The uncircumcised man in nature's state, who accomplishes the law, will judge you who are a transgressor of the law for all your written word and circumcision* (Ros. 2 : 27). It was possible, therefore, for a gentile under the Natural Law to be in God's grace.

The Speaker reveals that under the Mosaic Law he lost God's grace, by violating the commandment against desire; and he finds he cannot recover God's friendship, no matter how earnestly he wills to do so. The reason is that his faith is in the Law,— *You who seek justification through the Law have fallen away from grace. Christ will be of no avail to you.* It is impossible for a man to fulfil any obligation to God without grace. God will not accept, in fulfilment of an obligation, a purely natural action that has its source only in *the flesh*. The action must be supernaturalised; grace is the principle that supernaturalises, and Christ is the sole source of grace.

The Speaker, therefore, no matter how excellent his natural disposition is, no matter how ardently he wills it, cannot of himself (αὐτός 7 : 25) fulfil any of the obligations of the Law in which he seeks justification, because in adopting the Law, he is cut adrift from Christ and grace. He may actually fulfil the obligation as it is written in the Law, that is the letter of the Law, but it avails him nothing. *The will to do the good thing is there, but the doing is not there* (7 : 19). He is bound by every commandment of the abrogated Law; but because he is cut adrift from Christ, he gets no grace to fulfil them. Every commandment issues in sin. . . *the sinful passions aroused by the Law*. The Speaker is *sold away under sin*. Sin *lords it* over those living under the abrogated Law (Ros. 6 : 14).

Contrast this spiritual condition with that of Cain, who lived under the Natural Law: *but the lust thereof* (*sin*) *shall be under thee and thou shalt have dominion over it* (Gen. 4 : 7). The difference is that Cain is in contact by faith with the promised Redeemer, the *seed of the woman*. Authority and dominion over the lust of sin means that the sinner can resist sin in the first instance; and if he fails in the struggle, he can recover his loss, unless he wills it otherwise. He need never become the slave of sin. Surely men living under the Natural Law did not enjoy greater spiritual privileges in this basic human need than God's chosen people enjoyed under the Mosaic Law. Men living under the Natural Law were in a position to fulfil the obligations of the Law and become *just in God's sight* (Ros. 2 : 13). If we accept the commentators' interpretation of *Romans* VII we must admit that this was impossible under the Mosaic Law during its regime.

It is obvious from the internal evidence of chapter 7 : 7–25 that the incident portrayed there cannot belong to the period of the Law's regime, but to the regime of Christ when the Law was abrogated. When the Speaker cries out in despair, *who will release me from this body of death?*, the reply is given to him aside by St. Paul—*God through our Lord Jesus Christ*. Immediately the Speaker replies, *I give thanks to God through our Lord Jesus Christ*. This is the first time, apparently, he has heard of justification by God through faith in Christ. While living outside the Law, he was justified by the works of the Natural Law through faith in the promised Redeemer. In good faith he embraced the abrogated Law, thinking it was the Law of God, and like the Jews seeking justification through it; and he has told us of the consequences. Now he embraces the regime of Christ. *Now*, says St. Paul, *there is no condemnation against those in Christ Jesus. For the Law of the spirit, which is life in Christ, has freed you[1] from the law of sin and death* (Ros. 8 : 1). The law of sin and death is the abrogated Mosaic Law.

One Law in my members. . . . . .

Spiritual writers frequently quote the verse *one law in my members warring against the law of my mind and making me prisoner to the law of sin in my members* (Ros. 7 : 23), as signifying St. Paul's own struggle against the slavery of the flesh, "our woeful human servitude", as it has been called. These writers do St. Paul an injustice. This contest, of course, between the spirit and the flesh, has to be faced by every child of Adam; and the impenetrable armour supplied to mankind for the contest is faith in the Redeemer, faith in Christ, which saves man from defeat in the contest; and in case of defeat, rescues him from imprisonment by the law in the members. St. Paul knew this. The least of his disciples knew it.

When St. Paul refers elsewhere to the *thorn in the flesh*, which he says was given him by God as a curb of the pride that the wonderful favours he received might engender, I believe that he is referring to temptations of the flesh. St. Paul, like the other Apostles, was immune from sin, by virtue of his apostolic mission, but not immune from temptation. Commentators tell us, on the flimsiest evidence, that *the thorn* was some physical debility, disease of the eyes or epilepsy or some nervous disorder. It is most unlikely that Paul, destined as he was by Providence for the great mission to mankind, was ill-equipped in any department for the work on hand. There is no record that any one of the Twelve was so afflicted. The Christian Church, in selecting its missionaries, carefully scrutinises the health of the aspirant.

---

[1]*you* ($\sigma\epsilon$) is a better attested reading than *me* ($\mu\epsilon$). The version, *the law of the spirit of life in Christ* is incorrect. $\tau\hat{\eta}s$ $\zeta\omega\hat{\eta}s$ is genitive of definition or description.

Paul surely suffered from no infirmity that would make him an
object of pity or ridicule in the eyes of men. Physically, also, he
must have been a man of steel. Besides, he was not the man to
complain of mere physical inconvenience. He would have gloried
in it for Christ's sake. But he did fear, that while preaching to
others, he himself might become a castaway, rejected (1 Cor.
9 : 17). In the contest with the *thorn in the flesh, the messenger of
Satan,* Paul asked the Lord three times to put the adversary
away from him, *And he said to me, my grace is sufficient for thee*
(2 Cor. 12 : 7). Whatever the nature of the struggle, and it was
likely a spiritual one, St. Paul, unlike the Speaker in chapter VII,
knew where to apply for aid, and he was not disappointed. The
episode of chapter VII is not a record of the Christian's struggle
with temptation.

Where there is no Law, neither is there transgression

There remains to consider the six texts of St. Paul, which
according to Père Prat *condemn the Mosaic Law*, as being defective
from the beginning. *For where there is no Law neither is there
transgression* (Ros. 4 : 15). Commentators draw a strange distinction between sin and transgression. Before the Mosaic Law,
they argue, the sense of sin in general was dead, quoting *Romans*
7 : 9. St. Paul did not think so. After cataloguing the crimes of
the gentiles he says, *And yet they know the ordinance of God that
men who do such things are worthy of death. They not only do them,
but lend their approval to those who do them* (Ros. 1 : 32). Commentators render the statement of St. Paul, *the Law was added
on account of transgressions* (παραβάσεων χάριν Gal. 3 : 19), as
for the sake of transgressions, and interpret it : *what was only sin
before, now becomes a transgression,* being a violation of a positive
law. Now, every sin is a transgression of some law whether
natural, divine or human. But it does not follow that every transgression is a sin. The conditions of sin must be present. In ordinary
parlance sin and transgression are interchangeable terms. The
distinction made here by commentators is devoid of reality.

When St. Paul says in the text we are considering, that *where
there is no law there is no transgression* he is stating a truism.
Let us examine the context.

The Jews maintained that by virtue of the Mosaic Law they

and they alone were the heirs to the promise made to Abraham. St. Paul has been arguing that the promise had been in no way conditioned by the Law, which came some four hundred years subsequently. *If it were a case of heirs through observance of the Law, then Abraham's faith has gone for nothing and the promise has been voided. For law works wrath and where there is no law neither is there transgression* (Ros. 4 : 15). St. Peter himself admitted that the yoke of the Mosaic Law had been too much for themselves and their fathers to bear (Ac. 15 : 10). St. Paul's argument is, that it is recognised on all sides that the Jews have not observed the Law, and, therefore, if heirship depended on observance of the Law, their claim fails on that score. Then St. Paul adds the universalising statement about law in general. A law carries sanctions against transgression, *it works wrath.* The promise made to Abraham and *his seed* in return for his faith was unconditional, absolute. If the fulfilment by God of that promise had been dependent on the observance of a law by the heirs to the promise, then the result could well be the execution of sanctions for transgression of the law, not the manifestation of God's benevolence which the unconditional promise holds. A law of its very nature is calculated to provoke punishment and neutralise fulfilment of a promise conditional on the law's observance. An unconditional promise by God, on the other hand, is sure of fulfilment. No law, no transgression and no punishment. St. Paul is here dealing specifically with the promise to Abraham. It would be just as reasonable to interpret his statement on law as condemnatory of law in general as to argue, as Père Prat does, that in this passage St. Paul is condemning the Law of Moses during its regime.

The Law entered in that sin might abound

Père Prat and commentators generally, hold that the verse, *the Law entered in that sin might abound* (Ros. 5 : 20), refers to the giving of the Law to Moses in the first instance; and the purpose, or if not directly purpose, the inevitable result of its giving, we are told, was multiplication of sin, because the Law imposed precepts which were impossible to fulfil. Pharaoh very tyrannically commanded the Israelites under his dominion to make bricks, but supplied no straw from which bricks were made. If the commentators are correct in their interpretation of this verse of St.

Paul, Pharaoh's tyranny pales to insignificance before the tyranny of God, who imposed a law on the Israelites, a law of many precepts binding under the severest sanctions,[1] but incapable of fulfilment because that law lacked the grace necessary for fulfilment. Straw for making bricks could, at least in theory, be found somewhere. But God was the sole dispenser of the grace necessary to fulfil the Law, and we are told he withheld it. Yet the salvation of the Israelites depended on fulfilling the Law. Every instinct of fairplay in human nature revolts against such a monstrous imposition.

The Law, says Père Prat, *slipped slyly in behind original sin to come to its aid, and as a result we have the strange paradox,—the precept destined to give life ends up in death!* Père Lagrange rejects the Vulgate *subintravit* as a correct version of the Greek $\pi\alpha\rho\epsilon\iota\sigma\tilde{\eta}\lambda\theta\epsilon\nu$ (*entered in*). The Vulgate version implies, he says, secret underhand action, while there was nothing of that nature in the giving of the Law to Moses. Certainly not. Thunder and lightning are no allies of secrecy. But Père Lagrange falls into line with the other commentators in his interpretation of this text. So the position is this: We are told in *Leviticus* that the purpose of the Law was to make of the Israelites *a holy people, a priestly nation.* The instrument ordained by God to secure this end was the Mosaic Law. Moses himself applied all his energy and zeal to urge the people to keep the Law. The prophets, from Moses to Christ, spent themselves on the same mission. Christ himself emphasised the sanctity of even the least commandment, and castigated those leaders of Israel for making the fulfilment of the Law difficult (Mt. 23 : 23ff.). The commentators tell us that the purpose of the Law, at least the inevitable result of the Law, was to increase the number of sins, and to intensify the sense of sin. Thus people would realise the gravity of sin and become holy —sometime! Not of course in this life, for the precepts of the Law were binding on Israel from the cradle to the grave, and could never be fulfilled, according to the commentators.

There is no evidence for this theory of the Mosaic Law in the Old Testament. In fact if this theory of the Law were true the Old Testament would cease to have meaning. There is no evidence for it in the Gospels. If the Law could not be fulfilled

---

[1] *Every transgression, every disobedience incurred just retribution* (Hebr. 2 : 2).

for want of grace what was the sense of St. Stephen's rebuke to his executioners, *You are forever resisting the Holy Spirit as your fathers did . . . you also received the Law dictated by angels and did not keep it* (Ac. 7 : 51–3)? The sole source of evidence apparently is to be found in the Epistles of St. Paul, almost exclusively in the Epistle to the Romans. The commentators have misread St. Paul.

Let us examine this text *The Law entered in that sin might abound* (Ros. 5 : 20). In chapter v St. Paul is contrasting the damage done by Adam's fall with the benefits conferred on mankind by the man Christ. *Therefore just as through one man sin entered the world and through sin death, so death passed on to all men inasmuch as all men sinned* [*through Adam's sin*] (5 : 12). Christ is the second Adam bringing grace (*a gift*) where Adam brought sin. Only there is far more efficacy for good in Christ's gift, than for evil in Adam's sin. Adam's sin brought condemnation to all men *unto death. Christ's gift issues for all men in justification of their claim to life* (Ros. 5 : 18). Then the words are added *the Law entered in that sin might abound.* St. Paul means that the purpose of the Law in entering into the list, is to intensify the damage caused by Adam's fall. The contestants in the arena are Adam's sin on one side, Christ's gift on the other side. Now the Law enters in on the side of sin against Christ. But the commentators say that the text refers to the giving of the Law to Moses some thirteen hundred years before the coming of Christ. How do they propose to reconcile the context here with that theory? The context definitely shows that Christ has come, the second Adam, and delivered his gift, and at that stage the Law entered in to champion sin; and the obvious meaning is that the Mosaic Law, when set aside by the death of Christ, stealthily *sneaked in* (παρεισῆλθεν) on the side of sin against Christ. The vast majority of the Jews adhered to the abrogated Law, *a law of sin and death* at that stage, as St. Paul states in *Galatians* and demonstrated in *Romans* VII. The followers of the abrogated Law were the bitter enemies of Christianity. The Law on the side of sin *versus* Christ is the picture St. Paul paints, not the Law on the side of sin thirteen hundred years before Christ. A text should be read in its context.

Père Lagrange is correct in stating that the Law, in the first instance, was given publicly and solemnly, not, he says, in an underhand stealthy manner as the Vulgate *subintravit* suggests.

The use of the Greek word for *entered in* (παρεισῆλθεν) in this context is, he says, illustrated in Thucydides (2 : 59), describing the entry of Pericles to the assembly in Athens to address the people,—entering by the door (εἰσῆλθεν), passing up beside (παρά-) the audience on to the stage. The Vulgate (*subintravit*), however, is correct and is an exact rendering of the Greek word in the context.

The word in question (παρεισῆλθεν) is used only twice in St. Paul's Epistles; and according to the canons of exegesis, there is a strong presumption that a word used only twice by an author has the same connotation on each occasion, particularly if there is a very close resemblance between the contexts in which the word appears. Commentators agree that there are many points of close resemblance between *Romans* and *Galatians*, where this word also occurs (2 : 4). St. Paul tells of a visit from Antioch to Jerusalem— that described in Acts 15 : 2, which we have already mentioned,— when accompanied by Barnabas and Titus and *certain of the rest*, he went up to consult the Apostles in Jerusalem concerning the orthodoxy of his teaching and practice in the matter of circumcision and the Mosaic Law. The *certain of the rest* are false brethren belonging to the Pharisees, who proposed on this occasion at the Council of Jerusalem, that converts to Christianity must be circumcised, and referred particularly to Titus who was a Greek and uncircumcised. St. Paul describes these false brethren as *intruders who entered without authority* (παρεισῆλθον) *to spy on the freedom we have in Christ Jesus, in order to enslave us* (Gal. 2 : 4).

The question in discussion in *Galatians* was the abrogated Law of Moses, which those intruders who *entered without authority* were championing. Again, the matter in discussion in *Romans* 5 : 20 is the same abrogated Law of Moses, which after being set aside, goes over to the enemy, and contrary to every sense of duty and honour, enters the arena on the side of sin (παρεισῆλθεν). St. Paul describes the entry of sin itself as straightforward (εἰσῆλθεν). The *seed of the serpent* is entitled to its place in the arena against Christ; but the Law which was designed by God to sanctify his chosen people, has no authority to be there as an ally of sin. Like the intruders at the Council of Jerusalem, the abrogated Law also spied on the freedom of Christians by trying to impose its yoke on them *in order to enslave us*. The thought is thoroughly Pauline, and the text in its context presents no difficulty.

For through the Law is knowledge of sin

Another text from St. Paul relied on by Père Prat for his theory of the Mosaic Law is, *for through the Law is knowledge of sin* (Ros. 3 : 20). The Mosaic Law, he says, gives mankind a *clearer knowledge* of both original and actual sin. Will commentators, who agree with this view, not admit that original sin in Israelite infants was remitted by circumcision? That seems to be the generally accepted view of theologians. The commentators say that the Law during its regime pointed out sin but gave no grace to avoid it. In the case of circumcision then, the Law pointed out original sin to the eight day old child, but did nothing to remit it. Speaking to the Galatians, on whom the Judaizers tried to impose the abrogated Law, St. Paul says that circumcision now means nothing (Gal. 6 : 15). Did circumcision under the regime of the Law confer no spiritual benefits on Israelites? One wonders then why the child Christ was circumcised.

The text we are considering now *for through the Law is knowledge of sin* (Ros. 3 : 20), occurs in the following context. St. Paul has proved the universality of sin in the world. The sinfulness of the gentile world has been ruthlessly exposed. Quotations from the Old Testament prove the sinfulness of the Jewish world,—*we know that the words of the Law (the Old Testament) are meant for the Law's own subjects* (the Jews), *that all boasting may be stopped and that the whole world be proved subject to God's judgement* (3 : 19). That is, no man, Jew or gentile, can boast that he is not in need of justification by God. Then he adds, *because by the works of the Law no flesh shall be justified before him*, for *through the Law is knowledge of sin*. No man can say that he can justify himself by the works of the Law as it now stands, for the precepts of the Law cannot be observed and issue only in sin. And he continues, *but now (νυνὶ) without reference to the Law justification by God through faith in Christ is revealed* (3 : 20).

In the New Dispensation (νυνὶ) the Law is of no avail for justification, as is revealed in the Gospel. Justification now comes *without reference to the Law*. But it was not always so, *for Moses writes that the man who does the justice of the Law shall live thereby* (Ros. 10 : 5). *But now Christ has superseded the Law bringing justification to everyone who believes in him* (10 : 4). Under the Old Dispensation when the Law was in regime, men were justified by keeping the commandments of the Law. So said Moses, and St. Paul does not contradict him. So said Christ, and St. Paul does not contradict the teaching of Christ. But under the New Dispensation, the man who seeks justification through the Law is bound by all the commandments of the Law, and being cut away from Christ and grace, he can fulfil none of these commandments. For him the Law means *knowledge of sin*. This doctrine is enunciated by St. Paul in *Galatians* 5 : 4 and illustrated by a practical example in *Romans* 7 : 7–25. The text in question has no bearing on the Law during its period of regime. The context is justification under the New Dispensation as revealed in the Gospel.

Apart from the Law sin is dead

The verse, *Apart from the Law sin is dead* (Ros. 7 : 8), is quoted in support of the theory that the purpose of the Mosaic Law was merely to point out sin. "The Jew", we are told, "knew the will of God very clearly through the Law, but while the Law sharpened his moral judgement, it neither diminished the force of his concupiscence, nor gave him any special strength to live up to the more clearly known will of God." The Law pointed out sin but gave a man no help to avoid it. The Speaker in chapter 7 : 7 says that he did not know sin except through the Law. Outside the Law he lived a life of grace. He says that outside the Law he did not take cognisance of desire as a sin, and consequently the concupiscence of desire was dead in his case. But when the precept of the Law *thou shalt not desire* (*covet*) came, that particular concupiscence revived. The statement *apart from the Law sin is dead* refers to one particular form of sin or concupiscence. The statement is wrenched from its context and taken to mean every kind of sin or concupiscence. As I have already pointed out, St. Paul, dealing with the sins of the gentiles—those living *outside the Law*—clearly states that they realised the sinfulness of their actions, *for knowing the decree of God that men who do such things are worthy of death* (*that is spiritual death*), *not only do they do them but they lend their approval to those who do them* (Ros. 1 : 32). He speaks also of *the conscience of the gentiles bearing witness* to their moral obligations, as well as *their discussions among themselves defending or condemning* certain courses of action (Ros. 2 : 15). St. Paul actually says that it was *because of trans-*

gressions the Law was given, to isolate Israel from a sinful world (Gal. 3 : 19). Surely there was *knowledge of sin* before the Law was given to Moses.

Sin is not imputed where there is no law

It is argued, furthermore, that the expression *sin is not imputed where there is no law* (Ros. 5 : 13), points to the same conclusion, namely, that before the Mosaic Law, the sense of sin was largely dead because no positive law forbidding the sinful action existed. Therefore, it is said, the Mosaic Law can be truthfully described as *knowledge of sin*,—and nothing more. Again the context proves that the quotation from chapter v has no such meaning. The disaster inflicted on the human race by Adam's fall is contrasted with the benefit conferred on mankind by Christ's gift. Adam's sin brought death to all men. *Just as through one man sin entered the world and through sin death, so also death passed on to all men, inasmuch as all men sinned.* That is, in Adam's sin all men sinned and incurred the death sentence attached to Adam's sin, *for on what day soever thou shalt eat of it, thou shalt die the death* (Gen. 2 : 17). To prove that death is the penalty of Adam's sin, St. Paul continues: *For before the Law there was sin in the world, but sin is not imputed [for death] where there is no law [prescribing the death penalty]. But death reigned from Adam to Moses even against those who had not sinned after the manner of Adam's transgression* (Ros. 5 : 12-14). There was no law that prescribed the death sentence for sin between the days of Adam and Moses; and yet all the people of that period died, even though they committed no sin for which the death penalty was prescribed as in Adam's case. Therefore, death in their case was due to Adam's sin, not to any personal sin. After Moses, that is in the period of the Law, the death penalty was attached to several sins. The obvious meaning of the quotation is that when there is no law prescribing the death penalty for a sin, that sin is not reckoned for death. The word *law* here is used in its ordinary, general sense. It is not the Mosaic Law.

The sting of death is sin. The power for sin is the Law

Père Prat holds that the verse *the sting of death is sin, the power for sin is the Law* (1 Cor. 15 : 56) again refers to the union of original sin and the divinely appointed Mosaic Law *so that sin might abound*. St. Paul is speaking to the Corinthians about the Resurrection of the body: *This I tell you, brethren, that flesh and blood cannot win the kingdom of heaven, neither can corruption win incorruptibility* (1 Cor. 15 : 50). *Flesh and blood* means unaided sinful human nature, cut away from the Redeemer. *Corruption* means the condition of physical and moral depravation brought into the world by sin. St. Paul speaks of the *slavery of corruption* which befell irrational nature through Adam's sin (Ros. 8 : 21). St. Peter speaks of *the slaves of worldly corruption* (2 P. 2 : 19) whose lot is *darkness and gloom*. Then St. Paul proceeds: *For the trumpet will sound, and the dead shall rise immortal, and we shall be conformed*. The first personal plural *we* refers to those who die in Christ, united with Christ by faith. They will be conformed to the image of his glory. St. Paul is speaking here of the resurrection of the just. He quotes the prophet Osee, *where death is thy victory? where death is thy sting?* Death has no sting for the just who die in God's grace. They will rise immortal and glorious like the risen Christ. It is only those severed from God by sin, who will feel the sting of death. The Law is the power behind sin, *but thanks to God who gives us victory through Our Lord Jesus Christ*. It is the abrogated Law *versus* Christ. Adam's sin was the cause of death to all mankind, but the point at issue here, is the effect not the cause, of death. It is only for those who are estranged from God by personal sin that death retains its sting. They do not share in the fruits of Christ's victory over death, because sin stands in the way. And the Law is the power behind sin, *a law of sin and death*. There is no question here of original sin and the Law in question is the abrogated Law, the Law as it existed when St. Paul was writing to the Corinthians.

The Law abrogated in Christ

During his public life there is no record that Christ had at any time any quarrel with the divinely instituted Law of Moses. On the contrary, he speaks with marked reverence of the commandments of the Law, *but the man who keeps them and teaches others to keep them will be greatest in the kingdom of heaven* (Matt. 5 : 19). Why do commentators persist in saying that the divinely instituted Law during the period of its regime could not be kept? Like the

Jews, *no revelation tells them that it has been abrogated in Christ* (2 Cor. 3 : 14), and that St. Paul in his attacks on the Law is speaking not of the Law in regime but of the Law as abrogated in Christ, *the letter of the Law*, which was an immediate occasion of sin for those who sought for justification through it (Gal. 5 : 2).

It is, of course, admitted by all that the divinely instituted Law was powerless of itself to confer grace. *For owing to the impotence of the Law through its weakness in the hands of sinful nature, God sending his own Son in the likeness of sinful nature and to deal with sin, condemned sin through the [sinless] human nature [of Christ]* (Ros. 8 : 3). The Law itself was only an instrument in the hands of sinful human nature and of itself could never conquer sin. *If we can be justified through the Law then Christ's death was needless* (Gal. 2 : 21) said St. Paul to the Galatians, speaking of the abrogated Law, but that statement was true of the Law taken by itself alone, at all periods. Christ was the *raison d'être* of the Law. Divorced from Christ, the Law lost all its validity. Christ was the *end of the Law* (Ros. 10 : 4) in every sense of the term, and Christ made it clear that he himself had come to bring the Law to fulfilment (Matt. 5 : 17).

The Mosaic Law was given, as we have seen, to make of Israel *a holy nation* (Exod. 19 : 6). It was given *because of transgressions* not *for the sake of transgressions* as this phrase has been un- conscionably interpreted. The purpose of the Law was to preserve God's chosen people from the contamination of their neighbours and so to preserve the tradition of the worship of the one true God and to cherish the Messianic hope. For individual Israelites the Law was a "divinely authoritative guide to justice and life." "Not only was it (the Old Testament) the devout Israelite's religious history and law book, but also his prayer book and practical guide to life with its collections of beautiful hymns of praise and thanksgiving and written storehouse of divinely sanctioned maxims of the wise handed on for the guidance of future generations".[1] St. Paul, writing to Timothy who had been familiar with the books of the Old Testament from childhood, says: *They are able to make you wise unto salvation through faith in Christ Jesus* (2 Tim. 3 : 15). Without faith in Christ the Law was only a dead letter, a mere form of external ritualism against

---

[1] E. F. Sutcliffe, S.J., in *A Catholic Commentary*, 99d.

which the prophets ceaselessly warned Israel: *Doth the Lord desire holocausts and victims and not rather that the voice of the Lord should be obeyed?* (I Kgs. 15 : 22).

What was the effect of the Law on the life of Israel? *By their fruits you shall know them.* I shall quote the verdict of recognised authority: "A study of the religious history of this chosen race makes its election even more remarkable still, for its record through the pages of the Old Testament is largely one of backsliding and infidelity. Still with all its individual and even mass neglect of God the nation remained the one bright spot in the ancient religious world, where pure and true worship was at least the ideal proposed to all and at all times found faithful followers"[1] . . . . "In summary, Judaism did impose upon its followers a standard of morality which was far above anything in the world of its time. The average Jew was by all known standards a good man and a religious man . . . Judaism is a religion of external observance; but it also fostered a genuine interior piety unique in its time."[2]

Sanctity through the Law

Not only was it possible to observe the divinely instituted Mosaic Law, it was possible to attain to sanctity by its observance. "It is indeed true that in those of the just who lived before Christ, the Holy Ghost resided by grace, as we read in the scriptures concerning the prophets, Zachary, John the Baptist, Simeon and Anna; so that, on Pentecost the Holy Ghost did not communicate himself in such a way "as then for the first time to begin to dwell in the saint, but by pouring himself forth more abundantly; crowning not beginning his gifts, not commencing a new work but giving more abundantly" (St. Leo the Great hom. iii, de Pentec.). But if they also were numbered among the children of God, they were in a state like that of servants, *for as long as the heir is a child he differeth nothing from a servant, but is under tutors and governors* (Gal. 4: 1-2). Moreover, not only was their justice derived from the merits of Christ who was to come, but the communication of the Holy Ghost after Christ was much more abundant, just as the price surpasses in value

---

[1] *Id. ibid.*, 1115i.
[2] J. L. McKenzie, S.J., in *A Catholic Commentary*, 596d.

the earnest and the reality excels the image."[1] After stating that *the Law entered in to make sin abound* St. Paul immediately adds *but where sin abounded grace superabounded* (Ros. 5 : 21), referring to the activity of the Holy Spirit in the New Dispensation.

The theme of the *Epistle to the Romans* is that in the New Dispensation (3 : 21) salvation is secured through faith in Christ without reference to the Mosaic Law, as is revealed in the gospel. The Jews, for the most part, refused to accept Christ. He was not the Messias they wanted. *Israel in pursuit of a principle of justification failed to reach one, because it sought it not through faith in Christ, but through the works of the Law* (Ros. 9 : 31). Ignoring the justification that comes from God through faith in Christ, they tried to establish a justification of their own (10 : 3) by adhering to the Law, which was now cut adrift from the Redeemer, and was an instrument only of sin and death.

Efforts were made to enforce the Law on Christians, as being as essential to salvation in the new regime as it had been in the Old Dispensation. There is no indication in the *Epistle to the Romans* that the Judaizers were particularly active in the Roman Christian community. But wherever Jews lived in any considerable number, that danger was ever present. Besides his concern for the Roman Christians, St. Paul was deeply concerned for the great body of Jews who still adhered to the Law. St. Paul's love for Christ transcends every human emotion, and yet he says he could wish to be annihilated from before Christ's presence, if such an event could be of advantage to his countrymen (Ros. 9 : 3). As we have already argued, St. Paul hoped through this epistle to reach the minds and hearts of the great Jewish community in Rome, preparing the ground for the visit to which he looked forward impatiently.

The Jew who pleases God

The Jews believed it was sufficient for salvation to have Abraham as their father. St. Paul reminds them that God's choice of Abraham was an act of pure grace and that Abraham's children are those who, like Abraham, fulfil the divine will. Acceptance of Christ is no betrayal of Jewish traditions. The Mosaic Law is

[1] Quot. from Encyclical Letter of Pope Leo XIII for Pentecost 1897 published in *The Abiding Presence of the Holy Ghost in the Soul* by Bede Jarrett, O.P., p. 14.

obsolete and worthless. Faith in Christ was the spirit of the Law, nothing now remains but the letter. *It is not he who is a Jew in the eyes of men, nor yet the circumcision which is to be seen in the flesh: but it is he who is a Jew in his secret soul and it is circumcision of the heart through the spirit not through the letter,—that wins the praise not of men but of God* (Ros. 2 : 28–29).

The true Jew, one of God's chosen people, the Jew who is a child of Abraham and faithful to the noblest traditions of his race, is not he who has the outward marks of the Jewish nation nor he who parades his obedience to the Mosaic Law; but he who, like Abraham, rejoices to see the day of Christ, and has learned of Christ to be meek and humble of heart. With God the lot of such an one shall be glory; with men persecution, such as Paul himself endured. *If you belong to Christ then indeed you are Abraham's children. The promised inheritance is yours* (Gal. 3 : 29).

Chapter Eight

THE TEACHING OF CHRIST ON MARRIAGE AND DIVORCE

AMONG the ancient Israelites even pious persons practised polygamy. Jacob had Rachel and Zia as wives. Elcana, the father of Samuel, had two wives. Neither was David in the ranks of the monogamous. The Mosaic Law admitted polygamy. At least it provided for the disposition of the patrimony of a man with two wives (Deut. 21 : 15–17). Still, there seems to have been a feeling that monogamy was the higher state. Noe had only one wife. The prophets frequently represent God's relation with Israel in terms of marriage, Israel being the only nation with whom God had made a covenant. In the Book of Proverbs, too, monogamy seems to be the marriage ideal.

Divorce

In Deuteronomy it is prescribed that *if a man take a wife . . . and she find not favour in his eyes for some uncleanness, he shall write a bill of divorce, and shall give it in her hand, and send her out of his house* (24 : 1). Originally, the husband alone had the right to dissolve the marriage, but in later times this privilege was extended to the wife (Mk. 10 : 12). The Law denied the right of divorce to those guilty of certain misdemeanours before marriage (Deut. 22 : 13–29). Divorce, in all cases, was rendered more difficult for the poorer element of the population, inasmuch as the woman retained the right to her dowry.

St. Mark

At the time of Christ the rival schools of Shammai and Hillel disputed whether the *uncleanness* or *odious thing* that justified divorce, was shameful conduct on the woman's part, or merely some physical defect such as loss of comeliness or inability to cook or *any cause at all.* The school of Hillel stood for the liberal interpretation, which the strict Pharisees regarded as contempt of the Law. This explains their eagerness to embroil Christ in the controversy. Would he also support Hillel? Christ already had given proof of his contempt, according to their notions, for the Sabbath regulations; and his disciples ignored the fasting and ablution laws of the Pharisees. He had been known, too, to associate with publicans and people of doubtful moral character. Would he also ignore the precepts of the Law concerning marriage? So the Pharisees approached him *testing him: Is it lawful for a man to divorce his wife? He answered them, what command did Moses give you? And they said, Moses granted the privilege to write a bill of divorce and to divorce.* And Jesus answered them, *it was to meet your hardness of heart that Moses wrote you that commandment. From the beginning of creation God made them male and female. "For this reason shall a man leave his father and mother, and the two shall become one flesh." So that they are no longer two but one flesh. Therefore what God has joined together, let man not put apart* (Mk. 10 : 4–9).

His disciples evidently were surprised by Christ's reply. This apparently was the first time they had heard his teaching on marriage. Could there be any misunderstanding? St. Mark tells us that *back in the house again the disciples proceeded to question him further about this matter.* This doctrine of *one flesh* and *what God has joined together let man not put apart,* does it mean that the legislation of Moses is being set aside? Is it not permitted a man to divorce his wife? And Christ says to them: *whoever divorces his wife and marries another woman commits adultery against her (his wife); and if she divorces her husband and marries another man she commits adultery* (Mk. 10 : 12). We know from St. Matthew how the disciples reacted to this pronouncement.

Christ's teaching on marriage, as told in St. Mark's Gospel, is crystal clear. If the divorced parties, or either of them, should enter another marriage, it is adultery. Under the Mosaic Law divorce was granted in certain circumstances, and the marriage was dissolved. According to Christ's teaching divorce does not permit either party to enter a new marriage. Divorced though the husband and wife may be, they are still husband and wife, *one flesh.* Otherwise it would not be adultery for each or either of them to enter a new marriage. Divorce, therefore, in Christ's teaching, does not sever the marriage bond. It is not *divorce a vinculo*, such as obtained in the Mosaic Law. St. Mark does not state in what circumstances the divorce mentioned here is permissible. The emphasis is altogether on the indissolubility of marriage in the teaching of Christ. St. Matthew, in his account of this scene between Christ and the Pharisees, supplies us with further details.

St. Luke

The teaching of St. Luke's gospel is equally clear, beyond all controversy. *Every man who divorces his wife and marries another woman is an adulterer, and the man who marries a woman divorced from her husband is an adulterer* (Lk. 16 : 18). Again the emphasis is on the indissolubility of marriage. According to St. Luke also, a man may divorce his wife but may not marry another woman. That would be adultery in his case. The divorce in question does not dissolve his marriage with the woman whom he has divorced. She remains his wife, as is also clearly to be inferred from the latter part of the verse, *the man who marries a woman divorced from her husband is an adulterer*.

The setting in which St. Luke's doctrine appears is significant. He does not report Christ as *verbatim* quoting the decree of the Creator on marriage, but the context clearly indicates that it is the Creator's decree Christ is interpreting. *The Law and the prophets*—the Old Dispensation—(*was preached*) *until John. Since then it is the kingdom of Christ that is being preached and it is by violence to himself every man enters into it. But it is easier for heaven and earth to pass away than for one tittle of the Law to perish* (Lk. 16 : 16–17). Then follows immediately the teaching on marriage and divorce. What is the connexion in thought?

Under the Law and the prophets—in the Old Dispensation—dissolution of marriage was allowed by Moses *to meet the hardness of men's hearts*. In the New Dispensation, the Kingdom of God, that is being preached now, men will have to do violence to themselves, to deny themselves, if they are to become members of it. *If any man will come after me, let him deny himself. . . .* And yet the New Dispensation is the fulfilment or perfection, not the setting aside of the Old. Under the New Dispensation, marriage will be restored to the dignity ordained by God at creation. Divorce granting dissolution, which was a later concession to men's perversity, will be abolished. Christ's teaching on the indissolubility of marriage differs in no way from the doctrine of Genesis, *wherefore a man shall leave father and mother and shall cleave to his wife and they two shall become one flesh* (Gen. 2 : 24). The Law is not set aside. The exception to the Law is abolished.

St. Matthew

We have left St. Matthew's gospel until last, as it is only here that controversy arises: The first passage is verse 5 : 32 where Christ, in the Sermon on the Mount, is explaining the new spirit which must inspire his followers. *You have heard that it was said, thou shalt not commit adultery* (Mt. 5 : 27). But consent to the lust of evil desires makes a man an adulterer in his heart. *It was said, whoever divorces his wife, let him give her a bill of divorce. But I say to you that every man who divorces his wife, outside the case of unfaithfulness, makes her commit adultery, and whoever marries a divorced woman is an adulterer* (Mt. 5 : 32).

The more correct translation of this verse would be *makes for her committing adultery*. It does not necessarily follow that the divorced woman will commit the sin mentioned. Grammarians call this the tentative use of the verb ($\pi o \iota \epsilon \tilde{\iota}$). The teaching of Christ here is, that if a man divorces his wife for any reason other than that specifically mentioned, he exposes her to the danger of committing adultery. The divorced woman, therefore, is still married. Otherwise adultery would be out of the question. The divorce in question here cannot be such as dissolves the marriage bond. It is merely separation. The wife, short of the crime of unfaithfulness on her part, is entitled by the marriage contract to her husband's protection. Guilty, however, of unfaithfulness she has forfeited that right; and her husband, if he divorces her, is no longer guilty of exposing her to the danger of that sin.

According to St. Matthew's gospel (5 : 32) there is only one cause that would justify a husband in divorcing his wife, namely unfaithfulness on her part. According to St. Mark 10 : 12 an injured wife had the same right against an offending husband. It has been noted by commentators that the usual word for adultery is μοιχεία. The word πορνεία used here, and in verse 19 : 9, is of wider connotation still, and can present no difficulty in this context. It is rendered by *unfaithfulness*, and there is no doubt whatever about the meaning, as will be seen later.

Divorce a vinculo abolished

In Christ's teaching then, as expounded here, what provision is made for the case of a wife guilty of unfaithfulness? Under the Mosaic Law—*it has been said*—it was the husband's privilege to divorce such a woman, *to give her a bill of divorce* and turn her out of his house. Their marriage was dissolved, and each party was free to contract a new marriage. According to Christ's teaching a husband is still free to divorce a wife guilty of unfaithfulness. This conclusion is clearly to be inferred from verse 5 : 32. It is negative rather than positive teaching. Christ does not say, as the Mosaic Law said in effect, *if a wife is guilty of unfaithfulness, her husband shall divorce her*. The husband is free to follow his own will. But if he decides to divorce his guilty wife, is each party or either of them free to enter a new marriage? So it was under the Old Dispensation. What change has Christ introduced? *It was said . . . but I say to you*. This question is solved in the second part of verse 5 : 32. *And whoever marries a divorced woman is an adulterer*.

Is it not clear from this pronouncement that the old privilege has been taken away? St. Luke has it exactly the same, *the man who marries a woman divorced from her husband is an adulterer* (Lk. 16 : 18). What conclusion is possible from this teaching of Christ except that a divorced woman is still a married woman? She has a husband and neither of them may enter a new marriage while the other lives. Otherwise they are adulterers. Under the New Dispensation divorce is permissible, but marriage is indissoluble. Commentators gird at the exceptive clause *outside the case of unfaithfulness*. In the texts of Mark and Luke which we have examined, it is clearly stated that marriage in the New Dispensation is indissoluble. Is that doctrine not equally clearly stated in Matthew 5 : 32? The only additional information supplied by St. Matthew, is the cause which justifies divorce, unfaithfulness on the wife's part. But the divorce which is permissible in the circumstance does not sever the bond of marriage. *Whoever marries a divorced woman is an adulterer.* Though divorced she remains married.

St. Matthew verse 19 : 9 remains to be considered. At that time, we are told, Jesus had left Galilee and come into the part of Judea that lies byond the Jordan. This is the occasion described in St. Mark 10 : 1–12. St. Matthew gives more detail. The Pharisees came to him, *testing him* with the question, *is it right for a man to divorce his wife for any or every cause?* (κατά πᾶσαν αἴτιαν). The Pharisees, who posed as strict observers of the Mosaic Law, were hoping for an answer which would commit Jesus to the school of Hillel on this question. The followers of Shammai allowed divorce only on the grounds of the wife's unfaithfulness. If Jesus replied in the affirmative, it would be taken as further proof of his contempt for the Law. The Pharisees did not expect the reply they got, but they were probably no less pleased by it. A teacher who challenged the right of divorce, which was a privilege of Israel for over thirteen hundred years, was not likely to win popularity. The right to dissolve a marriage, when the wife was found unfaithful, was one of Israel's cherished ancestral customs.

Christ replied, *have you not read that the Creator made them from the beginning male and female and said, "for this reason shall a man leave his father and mother and cleave to his wife, and the two shall become one flesh"? So that they are no longer two but one flesh. What God therefore has joined let not man put apart.* The Pharisees retorted, *why then did Moses command to give a bill of divorce and to divorce?* Christ replied, *it was to meet your hardness of heart that Moses gave you the concession to divorce your wives. It was not so from the beginning. But I say to you that whoever divorces his wife not for unfaithfulness, and marries another woman is an adulterer. And the man who marries a divorced woman is an adulterer* (Matt. 19 : 3–9).

This is the famous pronouncement of Christ that has aroused so much controversy. The wording of it in Matthew's account is slightly different from that of Mark, and it is around Matthew's wording, the famous exceptive clause, *not for unfaithfulness,* the storm arose. Commentators refer to the "obscure exceptive clause", the "awkward negative" (μή) of verse 19 : 9. There is nothing awkward about the negative. It has exactly the same force as the word *outside of* (παρεκτός) of verse 5 : 32, only it is more classical. *Whoever divorces his wife* <u>*not*</u> *for unfaithfulness*—that is, for any cause other than unfaithfulness—*and marries another woman is an adulterer.*

We are justified, then, in inferring that a man may divorce his wife for unfaithfulness. He is free to do so. But if he divorces his wife for any other reason and marries another woman he is guilty of adultery. It would be fair also to infer from Christ's statement as it appears here in St. Matthew, that if a man divorces his wife for unfaithfulness and marries another woman he is not guilty of adultery. This indeed would be a fair inference from the first part of the verse if it were not immediately ruled out by the statement in the second part of the verse, *and the man who marries a divorced woman is an adulterer.* If this precise, direct and unqualified pronouncement of Christ were omitted from St. Matthew 19 : 9, then a case could be made for divorce *a vinculo* as far as this particular verse is concerned. Of course there still would be the evidence of St. Matthew 5 : 32 and St. Luke 16 : 18 where the same statement occurs. But as St. Matthew verse 19 : 9 stands it can never give comfort to the advocates of divorce *a vinculo.*

Evidence of the disciples

Furthermore, we have the evidence of those who were listening to Christ's doctrine on marriage on that occasion. The question of divorce was raised by the Pharisees, and we are not told how they reacted to Christ's reply. Probably they greedily seized on his teaching on marriage and divorce as further proof that he was an enemy of their Law. We are however explicitly told how the disciples of Christ reacted. They were his friends. They had been brought up under the Mosaic Law where the privilege of divorcing an unfaithful wife and marrying another was taken for granted, a privilege which, even on the strictest interpretation, Israel had enjoyed since the days of Moses. They heard Christ's preamble to the pronouncement when he claimed the authority of the Creator for the teaching he was about to impart . . . *no longer two, but one flesh. What God therefore has joined let not man put apart.* St. Mark, dealing with the incident, tells us that *back in the house the disciples questioned him further.* So that it is impossible that there could have been any misunderstanding on their part, when they declared *if the case of a man with his wife is so, it is better not to marry* (Mt. 19 : 10). Christ, of course, realised the meaning of this remark, but said nothing by way of correction. The disciples, therefore, understood that Christ's teaching on marriage had altered in a material way the conditions to which they were accustomed. *The man who marries a divorced woman is an adulterer* means that the privilege of divorce, as the disciples had known it, no longer obtains. A divorced woman, according to Christ's teaching, has a husband from whom death only can part her. It does not matter whether she was divorced legally or illegally, justly or unjustly. The statement is absolute and admits of no qualification. This is the meaning of the text as it stands, on its own merits in or out of its context. This was the understanding of the disciples who were listening to the pronouncement of Christ, and to whose ears this doctrine must have sounded revolutionary.

Why, then, has such controversy raged in modern times around these two texts of St. Matthew's gospel? For one reason, the translators have done St. Matthew injustice. All the English versions which I have seen, have mistranslated the latter part of verses 5 : 32 and 19 : 9. This is the Douai version of verse 5 : 32:

> *But I say to you that whoever shall put away his wife, excepting the cause of fornication, maketh her to commit adultery; and he that shall marry her that is put away committeth adultery.*

The advocates of divorce argue: He that shall marry her that is put away commits adultery, because she has been unjustly put away, *not for unfaithfulness*. Therefore she retains her married status. But if she were justly put away, they argue, she would lose her married status and could marry again. They argue, and quite legitimately as far as this English version goes, that the woman put away in the latter part of the verse is the woman of the first part of the verse, *her that is put away*.

The Revised Version: *But I say unto you that everyone that putteth away his wife saving for the cause of fornication maketh her an adulteress; and whoever shall marry her when she is put away committeth adultery.*

Here is the same confusion, *whoever shall marry her when she is put away* . . . clearly referring to the woman unjustly put away in the first part. If she were justly put away, it is claimed, she could remarry without guilt.

The Westminster version and the Knox version are after the same pattern,[1] all rendering the latter part of St. Matthew's verse incorrectly and failing to convey St. Matthew's meaning. One wonders had the translators the Greek before them. Or did they ignore St. Matthew's Greek and translate only from the Latin Vulgate? The key word in St. Matthew is ἀπολελυμένην. This is also the reading of St. Luke, and this reading has never been challenged by any critic. The versions quoted translate a reading τήν ἀπολελυμένην, which does not exist. *Hinc illae lacrymae.* The versions *her that is put away, her when she is put away, her after she has been put away,* are all obviously wrong. The absence of the definite article in St. Matthew and St. Luke makes all the difference. The English versions quoted emphasise the guilt of marrying *the woman (unjustly) put away.* The Greek original states the guilt of marrying *a woman put away,* and leaves no way of escape. The versions quoted can be legitimately interpreted as referring only to the individual woman mentioned in the first part of the verse. The Greek original is exhaustive in concept, *any* divorced woman, not *one* particular one. The Greek definite article—or rather, the absence of the definite article in the clause—serves to make this distinction quite clear. Latin, on the other hand, has no definite article, and the Vulgate *dimissam* can mean *the* divorced woman or *a* divorced woman. True to the heritage of original sin, the translators chose the wrong alternative.

The translators have made the same mistake in their version of St. Matthew verse 19:9, only here with more disastrous consequences. I shall quote the Knox version only. The others are of identical pattern. *And I tell you that he who puts away his wife, not for any unfaithfulness of hers, and so marries another, commits adultery; and he too commits adultery who marries her after she has been put away.* Again the same objection can be urged, more damaging now. The husband, it is argued, who puts away his wife for unfaithfulness does not commit adultery if he marries another. In the second part of the verse, it is claimed, the

---

[1] The New English Bible version, *And anyone who marries a woman so divorced commits adultery,* would be correct if *so* were omitted.

man who marries is guilty of adultery only because he marries a woman unjustly put away, *her after she has been put away*.

Some few editors omit the second part of the verse, Matthew 19 : 9, *the man who marries a divorced woman is an adulterer*, on the grounds of weaker manuscript authority here. All critics admit the authority of the half verse in Matthew 5 : 32 and Luke 16 : 18 in their record of the Sermon on the Mount, which was only a summary of Christian doctrine. It is most unlikely that this succinct statement on divorce was omitted on the particular occasion when Christ was professedly dealing with divorce in reply to the challenge of the Pharisees. Even though the half verse 19 : 9b had no manuscript authority in this particular connexion it is, none the less, Christ's teaching. Its validity as legislation does not depend on its context. If 19 : 9b were omitted, and if 19 : 9a were completely isolated from its context, and if it was the only existing evidence of Christ's teaching on the subject, then and then only could it be inferred that Christ's legislation made no change whatever in the divorce regulation that obtained in the Mosaic code, namely that violation of marriage vows justified the dissolution of marriage.

A new interpretation

In a recent publication[1] the exegesis is defended which sees no exception whatever in Matthew 5 : 32 and 19 : 9. The clauses generally rendered, *outside the case of unfaithfulness* and *not for (except for) unfaithfulness* are given an entirely different meaning. The term πορνεία, usually rendered *unfaithfulness*, is claimed to mean *concubinage* or *prostitution*, referring particularly to incestuous unions which were forbidden by the Mosaic code (Levit. 18 : 1–17). Christ's purpose, we are told, in introducing this matter to his legislation on marriage and divorce, is to warn that under the New Dispensation also, these incestuous unions are forbidden.

This interpretation is defended by Père Bonsirven. His version of 5 : 32 is: *whoever sends away his woman (except in case of prostitution) makes her commit adultery;* while he renders 19 : 9, *whoever sends away his woman (not being in state of prostitution)* . . . These incestuous unions were not marriages. The parties

---

[1] *Le Divorce dans le nouveau Testament*, J. Bonsirven, S.J. Paris 1948.

were living in concubinage. Hence Père Bonsirven avoids the words *wife* and *divorce;* because these terms are applicable only to regular valid marriage; but *sending away* he takes in the full sense of permanent separation, dissolving the union. The meaning then is: Under the New Dispensation a man cannot send away his woman unless she is living with him in a state of prostitution ($\pi o \rho \nu \epsilon \acute{\iota} a$) or concubinage. In that case he is bound to send her away.

The reasons put forward by Père Bonsirven in defence of this view are: to avoid contradiction or the semblance of contradiction, in Christ's teaching; to avoid exception or apparent exception to the law forbidding *divorce a vinculo;* to avoid the linguistic and grammatical difficulties inherent, it is claimed, in the generally accepted version.

Let us deal first with the linguistic and grammatical difficulties. It is claimed that in the New Testament the term signifying adultery is invariably $\mu o \iota \chi \epsilon \acute{\iota} a$ not $\pi o \rho \nu \epsilon \acute{\iota} a$, as this text of St. Matthew has it. In the New Dispensation adultery, as we interpret the text, is a justifying cause for separation or divorce *a mensa et thoro*, and the specific meaning of $\mu o \iota \chi \epsilon \acute{\iota} a$ is adultery. But there were and are, other justifying causes (of the same genre) for separation besides formal adultery—the sexual sins against nature mentioned in *Romans* 1:26–27; the heinous crime mentioned in Leviticus 18:23. These and such crimes are classed under the generic title of *sexual debauchery*, and this is the exact meaning of $\pi o \rho \nu \epsilon \acute{\iota} a$ in St. Matthew's text, a recognised meaning in the New Testament. The term, of course, has also a specific signification. It can be taken that $\pi o \rho \nu \epsilon \acute{\iota} a$ was used purposely by St. Matthew to cover cases which would not fall under the connotation of $\mu o \iota \chi \epsilon \acute{\iota} a$, and the version *unfaithfulness*, signifying sins against the marriage vow, is a fair rendering.

Exception is taken also to the meaning assigned in the accepted version to the negative $\mu \acute{\eta}$. It is said that $\mu \acute{\eta}$ by itself never characterises an exception, $\epsilon \acute{\iota}$ or $\dot{\epsilon} \acute{a} \nu$ being necessary for this purpose. But the text of St. Matthew reads $\ddot{o}s \ \ddot{a} \nu \ \dot{a} \pi o \lambda \acute{\upsilon} \sigma \eta \ \ldots \ \mu \acute{\eta}$. Surely it is not necessary to repeat $\ddot{a} \nu$ ($\dot{\epsilon} \acute{a} \nu$) immediately before $\mu \acute{\eta}$. And if $\mu \acute{\eta}$ here is separated from the verb and attached immediately to the word or clause it governs ($\mu \acute{\eta} \ \dot{\epsilon} \pi \grave{\iota} \ \pi o \rho \nu \epsilon \acute{\iota} a$), this is quite a regular practice. The emphasis is thrown on the operative word or clause. It can be rendered by an italicised *not*.

Again, the claim that ἐπὶ with the dative does not designate the cause assigned for an action (*because of unfaithfulness*) will be found altogether invalid. It may be taken that the Greek of Matthew 19 : 9a, as rendered in the accepted version, is above reproach, worthy even of Demosthenes. The half verse states exactly what it wants to state, namely that in certain circumstances separation is tolerated in Christian marriage. Any damaging inference that could be drawn from the half verse if isolated, is ruled out by the context, as we have already explained.

On the other hand, the interpretation we are considering, is entirely unwarranted by the context. The field of discourse is marriage, valid marriage and divorce. These incestuous unions in question were not marriage unions. The description *what God has joined together* does not fit them. They were condemned even by the Natural Law, which remains in force in the New Dispensation. It is extremely doubtful if the meaning suggested in this interpretation can be wrested from the Greek without violence to language and syntax. This interpretation, furthermore, leads to confusion and contradiction. How is it proposed to render Matthew 19 : 9b which is identical with 5 : 32b? To be consistent, the version must run thus: *The man who marries a woman who has been sent away is an adulterer.* But if the woman sent away is not a married woman, but one living in prostitution, there is nothing to prevent her from marrying. Marriage and non-marriage cannot be treated indiscriminately under the same heading.

Critics have animadverted on the circumstance that while Matthew and Mark record the teaching of Christ on marriage and divorce, when he was challenged by the Pharisees, Mark is altogether silent on the matter of unfaithfulness. Perhaps "altogether silent" is an overstatement. Mark tells us that *when they were back in the house his disciples questioned him further on this matter* (10 : 11). St. Matthew was writing for Jews in whose eyes violation of the marriage vow on the part of the woman, deserved death and called for immediate dissolution of the marriage. So the Mosaic Law ordained. Naturally, Jews wanted to know how the case stood in the New Dispensation. St. Mark was writing for Roman gentiles, in whose estimation unfaithfulness was just one of the hundred and one pleas that secured dissolution from the civil court. The mere whim of the parties was sufficient. Christ's legislation, of course, bound all alike Jew and gentile.

Apparently, too, from the beginning married Christians availed themselves of the permission to separate in certain circumstances. St. Paul, writing to the Corinthians some twenty-five years after the death of Christ, says: *To the married I give command—not I but the Lord—that a wife is not to separate from her husband. But if she has separated, let her remain so without marriage, or become reconciled to her husband. And that a husband is not to put away his wife* (1 Cor. 7 : 11) . . . St. Paul says this is the teaching of Christ. Where in the gospel, if not in these two verses of St. Matthew (5 : 32; 19 : 9), can it be said that Christ tolerated separation?

Christ's teaching on marriage and divorce is contained in three brief articles within the comprehension of the least sophisticated intellect: (i) *The two are in one flesh*—Christian marriage is monogamous, one husband and one wife. (ii) *What God has joined together let not man put apart*—Christian marriage is a sacrament, not a merely human contract; and can be set aside, by no human authority. (iii) *The man who marries a divorced woman is an adulterer*—the divorce tolerated in Christian marriage does not break the marriage bond.

Chapter Nine

THE TRIUMPHANT ENTRY INTO JERUSALEM

This made the Jews more determined than ever to kill him, that he not only broke the Sabbath, but spoke of God as his own father, making himself as equal to God (Jn. 5 : 18).

AT the feast of the Tabernacles the chief priests and Pharisees sent officers to arrest Jesus (Jn. 7 : 33). But the officers returned without him, saying *Nobody has ever spoken as this man speaks.* Subsequently the Jews, enraged by his reference to Abraham, took up stones to cast at him, *but Jesus hid himself and went out of the temple* (Jn. 8 : 59).

Again at the feast of the Dedication, *as he was walking about in the Temple, in Solomon's porch* the Jews gathered around him and said *how long wilt thou go on keeping us in suspense? If thou art the Christ tell us openly* (Jn. 10 : 24). Jesus ended his reply to them by saying *the Father and I are one* (10 : 30). Again the Jews took up stones to stone him. Jesus asked them for which of the many deeds of mercy he had done in their midst they were stoning him. The Jews answered, *it is not for any deed of mercy; it is because thou who art a man, art making thyself out to be God* (Jn. 10 : 33). Again Jesus escaped from their midst and *went back to the other side of the Jordan, to the place where John was when he first baptised* (Jn. 10 : 40).

The raising of Lazarus from the dead may be regarded as the first scene of the dramatic entry into Jerusalem on the first Palm Sunday. It was at the place here indicated, *on the other side of the Jordan*, that the messengers announcing the illness of Lazarus reached Jesus. And Jesus, on hearing the message, said, *the end of this sickness is not death; it is meant for God's honour, to*

bring honour to the Son of God (Jn. 11 : 4). And later, *Lazarus
is dead. For your sakes I am glad I was not there, so that you may
believe* (11 : 15).

Against the protests of his disciples Jesus resolved to return
to Judea two days after receiving the message, but he delayed
purposely to heighten the significance of the miracle he had in
mind to perform. When he arrived in Bethany he found that
Lazarus had been four days in the tomb. As Bethany was less
than two miles from Jerusalem, a number of Jews from Jerusalem
had gone out to sympathise with the sisters of Lazarus.

On the approach of Christ, Martha went out to meet him and
said, *Lord, if thou hadst been here my brother would not have died.
Even now I know that God will grant thee whatever thou dost ask
of him* (Jn. 11 : 22). Martha had known of cures effected by Jesus,
of cases even where the dead had been restored to life. But
these had been only a short time dead. The mourners were still
around the dead body of Jairus's daughter (Mt. 9 : 24). The son of
the widow of Naim was being borne out to the tomb (Lk. 7 : 12).
The Jews buried their dead on the day of death. Martha, aware
that her brother was now four days in the tomb and that putrefac-
tion must now be setting in, hesitated about making a direct
request. Still she was aware of Christ's power and made a perfect
act of faith in his divinity, *I believe that thou art the Christ the Son
of God, the one due to come into the world* (Jn. 11 : 28).

Before performing the miracle Jesus prayed aloud to the Father:
*Father, I thank thee for hearing my prayer. For myself I know that
thou hearest me at all times. But I say this for the sake of the crowd
that is standing around, that they may believe it is thou who hast
sent me* (Jn. 11 : 2). As St. John says further on, *Jesus knew well
that the Father had left everything in his hands; knew it was from
God he came and to God he was going* (Jn. 13 : 4). He is now publicly
claiming the authority of God the Father for the miracle he is
about to perform, that the onlookers may have evidence for
believing that he is truly the Son of God. Many of the Jews, we
are told, who had visited Martha and Mary and had seen what
Jesus did, believed in him (Jn. 11 : 47). *Indeed that was why
the multitude went out to meet him* (*on Palm Sunday*), *because they
had heard of his performing this miracle* (Jn. 12 : 18). Some also
who witnessed the miracle hastened to denounce Christ to his
enemies.

This great miracle led directly to the signing of Christ's death warrant. The chief priests and Pharisees summoned a council at which Caiphas the high priest proposed, with unconscious prophecy, that it was expedient that one man should die for the sake of the people. *From that day forward they plotted his death* (Jn. 11 : 53).

Return to Jerusalem

Immediately after the miracle, Jesus withdrew from the neighbourhood of Jerusalem to the little town of Ephrem, *near the desert*. The Jews were probably glad to be rid of him for the moment. They would deal with him later after the Paschal celebrations. But the course of Christ's actions was not to be dictated by his enemies. Now, contrary to all human notions of prudence, at the moment when the hatred of his enemies had reached its climax, Jesus decides to enter publicly into Jerusalem, the stronghold of his enemies; not only that, but to claim as Messias, that the city was his royal capital and to enter in state as its acknowledged King.

Jerusalem was the capital of the Messianic kingdom. *The law shall come forth from Sion, and the word of the Lord from Jerusalem* (Is. 2 : 2–4). On the occasions of the Nativity, Baptism and Transfiguration Christ's divinity had been proclaimed from heaven. St. Peter, speaking for the Apostles, had solemnly confessed his faith in the Messias, *the Christ, the Son of the living God* (Mt. 16–17). The evil spirits driven forth in exorcism had confessed his Messiaship, *but he rebuked them and would not have them speak, because they knew that he was the Christ* (Lk. 4 : 41). Throughout his ministry Christ studiously avoided public recognition as the Messias. The popular notion of the kingdom which the Messias was to establish needed drastic correction. Now, however, with less than one week of life left, the time had come to fulfil the prophecy of Zachary:

> Rejoice greatly O daughter Sion,
> Shout for joy O daughter Jerusalem
> See your king is coming to you.
> He is just, he is your Saviour
> Humble, riding on an ass that has borne the yoke
>   and upon a colt her foal.

(Zach. 9 : 9.)

The time had now come for the people of the kingdom to proclaim their king and publicly confess their loyalty to him, acknowledging him as the Messias. Even during the Feast of the Tabernacles, *for fear of the Jews nobody dared to speak of him openly* (Jn. 7 : 13). The hatred and opposition in Jerusalem had been intensified by the miracle at Bethany. Yet Jesus, completely ignoring his enemies, makes the momentous decision to enter the city as its King, as one invested with complete authority and supreme control of the city. There is no attempt at secrecy. Everything takes place in the broad light of day. Yet beyond a feeble even reverent protest on the part of the Pharisees no voice or hand is raised in opposition. Christ for the moment asserts his supreme lordship. His will is paramount. When the time comes—and the initiative in this matter also lies with him,—he will accept imprisonment and death.

The Lord hath need of them

The triumphant entry into Jerusalem is recorded by all four Evangelists, St. John, however, supplying details which are absent in the other gospels. *Six days before the paschal feast Jesus went to Bethany* (Jn. 12 : 1). Here Christ and his disciples attended a feast at which Lazarus was present, and where the anointing by Mary, the sister of Lazarus, took place. Bethany, on the eastern slope of Mt. Olivet, is less than two miles from Jerusalem. Here, we may take it, the party rested for the Sabbath. On Sunday morning Christ and his disciples set out for Jerusalem. On the outskirts of the village of Bephthage, on the road to Jerusalem, he sent two of his disciples on an errand: *Go into the village that is opposite you and immediately you will find an ass tethered and her foal with her. Loosening them bring them to me. And if any one says anything to you, say "the Lord hath need of them." Immediately he will despatch them* (Mt. 21 : 2–3). Mark (11 : 2) and Luke (19 : 13) speak only of a colt foal which nobody had yet ridden. John says nothing about the instructions to the two disciples, merely, *taking an ass's foal he mounted on it* (12 : 14).

Commentators are not agreed on the exact wording of Christ's message to his two disciples on this occasion. Though the point at issue is only a matter of detail, still the solemnity of the occasion invests the smallest detail with significance. Some commentators hold—it seems to be the modern tendency—that the explanation which was to be given to anybody challenging the taking away of the asses was: *the Lord hath need of them and he (the Lord) will return them immediately*. An assurance to the owner that his property will be returned, sounds rather commonplace in this context, where generally the element of coincidence scarcely succeeds in explaining events. Some commentators even suggest that everything had been prearranged with the owner of the asses. It is much more in harmony with the context here to interpret Christ's words of explanation to anybody who might challenge, as *the Lord hath need of them*. That is, the very mention of the title Lord will be sufficient guarantee that his will on this occasion will be instantly executed. The Lord is God before whose eyes all things are present and whose *fiat* is instantly accomplished. He tells the messengers where they will find the mounts for the royal procession, and his words imply that the mention of the Lord having need of them, will be guarantee of the owner's immediate surrender of them.

The form of the message in St. Mark's gospel bears out this view. Whereas St. Matthew uses the future (ἀποστελεῖ), *he will despatch them*, St. Mark uses the present tense (ἀποστέλλει), indicating immediate future certainty, *and immediately he (the owner) despatches them back here*. That is, the owner no sooner hears of the Lord's need, than he releases his property. There is no break in the continuity of time such as the future suggests. Besides, and this is significant, St. Luke tells us the disciples were actually challenged by the owner, *why are you untying the colt?* The reply is *because the Lord hath need of him*. There is not a word about returning the property. Furthermore it will be found that the Greek ἀποστέλλειν always connotes *sending out* on a message or mission, never *sending back*. It is the word used here by the three Synoptists to describe the sending of the messengers on this particular mission. It also describes the action of the owner of the asses despatching his property to take part in the royal procession.

There is a further point that worries some commentators, the discrepancy between St. Matthew and the other Evangelists on the number of asses. St. Matthew mentions two, the others only one. A commentator mentions " the absurdity of a rider using two

mounts apparently at the same time." Another commentator
suggests that the dam was brought in order to coax the colt foal
to go quietly. The truest commentary might be that St. Matthew
mentions two asses *in order that the scripture might be fulfilled.*
We sometimes read of an important person entering a city riding
in a carriage and four. The obvious meaning is that the carriage
was drawn by four horses. Zachary who lived five hundred years
before the event, visualised two asses in the royal procession to
Jerusalem. We know from the Evangelists Mark and Luke that
the King rode the colt that had never before been ridden. St.
Matthew tells us that the disciples placed their garments, by way
of saddling, on the animals. We are surely justified in inferring
that the royal mount was led by one of the disciples who had
carried out the message, probably St. Peter; while the second
mount, saddled but riderless, was led by the other disciple
probably St. John. The King, riding into his capital on this great
occasion, would not be left without escort.

The Prince of peace

The King in question is the Prince of peace. *He will do away
with Ephraim's chariots and Jerusalem's warhorses. He will do away
with the bows of war and bestow peace on the nations . . . and his
sway will be from sea to sea*, continues Zachary in this context
(9 : 10). The humble ass was the symbol of peace. The Lawgiver
had warned Israel's kings not to retain a multitude of horses,
since they must not set their hearts on military campaigns
(Deut. 17 : 16). Isaias had deplored the fact that the land was
full of horses and chariots, with the result that men forgot God
(Is. 2 : 7).

Scenes like the present one, had occurred at the enthronement
of Jehu . . . *and taking everyman his garment laid it under his
feet . . . and they sounded the trumpet and said Jehu is king*
(4 Kgs. 9 : 13). And again at the entry of Simon Machabaeus into
Jerusalem . . . *with thanksgivings and branches of palm trees*
(I Mach. 13 : 51).

The procession started on the outskirts of Bephthage when
the disciples returned with the asses which they found where
Christ had indicated, tied at the entrance of the village, *to a gate
outside in the laneway* says St. Mark (11 : 11) who, doubtless, got

the detail from St. Peter, himself, probably an eyewitness. Christ had told his disciples nothing of the significance of the great occasion, when he was to be publicly acclaimed as the Messias. It was *only after Jesus had attained his glory*, says St. John, that the disciples realised *what they had done, and how it fulfilled the words written of him* (12 : 16).

But secrecy was not the motive of Christ's silence on the occasion. When at the beginning of this journey to Jerusalem he cured the blind man on the outskirts of Jericho, who appealed to him for pity as *Jesus, Son of David*, Jesus gave him back his sight, but contrary to his previous custom imposed no command of silence on him. The man followed him glorifying God (Lk. 18 : 42–3).

Those who went out from Jerusalem to meet the royal procession were, apparently, all strangers in Jerusalem. Were the natives, even those who believed in him, afraid to be seen in his company? There were *many from the country who went up to Jerusalem to purify themselves before paschal time began* (Jn. 11 : 55). Evidently they were disciples. *They were looking for Jesus*, we are told, standing around in knots in the Temple and saying to one another, *"what do you think? He will never come to the feast, will he?"* They were hoping against hope. They realised the intensity of hatred that followed on the miracle at Bethany and they could scarcely believe that, in face of such opposition, Jesus would dare to come to Jerusalem for the festival. *The chief priests and Pharisees had given orders that any one who knew where he was should report it to them so that they would arrest him* (Jn. 11 : 56). Now the wanted man was coming of his own accord; not only that, but coming in royal estate to take possession of his capital, surrounded by his subjects enthusiastically proclaiming their allegiance.

These pilgrims from the country, hearing that Christ was coming, left Jerusalem on Sunday morning to meet the procession, and when they met the royal party, turned to lead the procession, strewing the way with palm branches. St. Matthew (21 : 9) and St. Mark (11 : 10) speak of *the multitudes that went before and followed after him crying aloud Hosanna for the Son of David.* St. John says *there were many who had been with him when he called Lazarus out of the tomb . . . and these, too, bore witness to him* (12 : 17). St. Luke says *the whole company of his disciples began rejoicing and praising God for all the miracles they had seen* (19 : 38).

The processionists, then, we may take it, were all disciples whose faith in the divinity of Christ had been sealed by the miracle of the raising of Lazarus, whether they had witnessed the miracle or merely heard of it. Their faith was fervent and their hosannas sincere. The country folk who came out from Jerusalem knew of the bitterly hostile attitude of the Pharisees, but consideration of personal safety did not prevent them from leading the royal procession into the enemies' stronghold. The disciples who followed knew what they had to expect in Jerusalem. Referring to the first stage of the journey from their retreat near the desert St. Mark says, *and Jesus went before them and they were astonished . . . and following were afraid* (10 : 32).

Commentators frequently animadvert on the fickleness of the people who cried hosannas on Sunday, and the following Friday shouted *away with him, crucify him:* "There could be no doubt of the burning enthusiasm of these people, but it was ill-informed and national rather than religious in character." This explanation seems scarcely adequate. St. Matthew tells us of the reaction in Jerusalem when the royal procession entered: *the city was shaken to its depth* (πᾶσα . . . ἐσείσθη 21 : 10). This description indicates the impact of an event catastrophic in its unexpectedness. How did it happen that Jerusalem was completely taken by surprise in this manner? St. John tells us that there were many Jews in Jerusalem who were going over and believing in Jesus (12 : 11). A great number of them had gone to Bethany when they heard that Christ and his disciples were there. They went out *not only on account of Jesus, but to have sight of Lazarus* (Jn. 12 : 9). They probably had returned to the city before the Sabbath began. Many of the rulers, we are told, *believed in him, but they would not profess it because of the Pharisees, afraid of being expelled from the Synagogue* (Jn. 12 : 43).

One wonders what part the city folk played on this occasion. Did those who believed in Jesus, fall in with the procession and join in the applause? On the occasion of the feast of Tabernacles they were afraid to be heard mentioning his name (Jn. 7 : 13). We may take it that the vast majority of the city inhabitants were non-believers: *Such great miracles he did in their presence and still they did not believe in him* (Jn. 12 : 37). St. Matthew tells us that in the first moments of commotion people asked *who is this?* And the crowds said *this is the prophet Jesus from Nazareth of*

Galilee—the crowds, that is, that happened to be present at
every vantage point or street crossing where the question was
asked. Their reply shows that they had no faith in Christ as
Messias. He is just the prophet from Nazareth. Jerusalem had
been accustomed to prophets and had an evil reputation as the
death place of prophets, and in the course of a few days would give
further and final proof that the present generation was not un-
worthy of its forbears. Did the indifferent, unbelieving crowds
now look on in open-mouthed astonishment, hushed to a reverent
silence? They surely did not join in the hosannas to the Son of
David. Yet not a hand or voice was raised against Christ or his
followers, beyond a feeble and now respectful protest from the
Pharisees.

Jesus in the Temple

Yet, it was not an event of whirlwind suddenness that was over
before people could recover from the first shock of surprise.
Jesus went into the Temple, St. Matthew tells us, *and drove out
from it all those who bought and sold there and overthrew the tables
of the bankers . . . and there were blind and lame who came up to him
in the Temple and he healed them there* (21 : 12–14) . . . The
Baptist sent two of his disciples from his prison to inquire *art
thou he who is to come or are we to expect another?* And Jesus
answered, *tell John . . . the blind see and the lame walk . . .*(Lk.
7 : 22). Healing the afflicted was to be one of the functions and
prerogatives of the Messias.

The chief priests and scribes saw the miracles that he did now
and saw and heard the boys that cried aloud *hosanna for the Son
of David.* But beyond a respectful protest they controlled their
rage. *Dost thou hear what they are saying?* they reverently protested.
Did the boys understand the significance of their hosannas for the
Son of David? The chief priests and scribes understood *and they
were greatly angered at it.* On one occasion Jesus had asked the
Pharisees, *What is your opinion concerning Christ? Whose son is
he to be? They told him David's* (Mt. 22 : 42). Now there is no
rushing for stones as on the occasion of the Dedication festival,
because being man he made himself out to be God. Christ's reply
to the Pharisees' suggestion to silence the children was not
calculated to ease their discomfiture. Quoting their beloved Law

he said, *have you never read the words, "out of the mouths of babes
and sucklings thou hast wrought a hymn of praise"*? The babes and
sucklings in the Temple acclaimed Christ as the promised
Messias, *the Son of David*.

Earlier in the day some of the Pharisees who heard the hosannas
for the Son of David, for the King of Jerusalem who was coming,
said to him respectfully, helplessly: *Master, rebuke thy disciples*,
and Jesus replied: *I tell you if they should keep silence the stones
will cry out instead* (Lk. 19 : 39–40); that is, if on this unique
occasion rational creation should fail to recognise and acclaim
Christ as the Messias, the promised Saviour of the world, then
Christ himself, the Lord of creation, will endow mute and lifeless
nature with voice to proclaim aloud the great truth.

On the occasion of his triumphant entry into Jerusalem, Christ's
divinity was publicly confessed throughout the streets of the
capital as genuinely and sincerely as his divinity was confessed
by Martha immediately before the raising of Lazarus. If one
stops to inquire how this event could have happened in the very
stronghold of his enemies whose implacable hatred would be
registered on Calvary's hill in the course of a few days, the only
possible explanation seems to be that of the Master himself when
sending his two disciples on the first errand in connexion with
the procession—*the Lord has need of it*. The Lord's will is supreme
and no opposition can thwart it. The prophecy of Zachary must
be fulfilled, *See your king is coming to you . . . and he rides upon
an ass*. He was coming as the Prince of peace, *to bestow peace upon
the nations*, and his official entry into his capital was not to be
marred by a single word or act of violence, because the Lord
hath need of it. He chose the present occasion for the celebration
of this event, much to the disappointment of the Sanhedrin. The
Passover was the oldest feast observed by God's chosen people.
It commemorated the release of Israel from the bondage of Egypt.
The blood of the lamb sacrificed at Goshen preserved Israel
from death and opened the way to freedom. In the Passover
now being celebrated, symbol would yield to reality. *Our paschal
lamb Christ is immolated*, the Church sings in her Easter Preface.
By his death voluntarily accepted at the time he willed, Christ
delivered mankind from the bondage of Satan.

The salutations of the processionists who preceded and followed
Christ on his triumphant entry to Jerusalem indicate clearly that

they believed he was the Messias, the promised Saviour of mankind, *the one destined to come. Son of David* was the most popular Messianic title. Israel believed that the promised Messias would be descended from the royal house of David. When Christ cured the man possessed, who was dumb and blind, *the multitudes were filled with amazement. Can this*, they asked, *be any other than the Son of David* (Mt. 12 : 23). The Angel Gabriel announcing to Mary that she was to be the Mother of the Saviour said, *the Lord will give him the throne of David his father* (Lk. 1 : 32). *He shall sit on the throne of David* (Is. 9 : 7). The prophecy of Zachary is now fulfilled.

The title of Lord

The title however of supreme honour given to Christ on this occasion is that of Lord. *Blessed is he who comes with the title of Lord* (ἐν ὀνόματι κυρίου). *Blessed is he who comes as King with the title of Lord* (Lk. 19 : 38). *Blessed is he who comes with the title of Lord and King of Israel* (Jn. 12 : 13). Commentators generally translate this phrase *in the name of the Lord*. But this version greatly minimises the significance of the salutation. Every prophet came in the name of the Lord and spoke as the mouthpiece of the Lord. Even the unbelieving hostile crowds in Jerusalem who described him as *the prophet from Nazareth in Galilee* would admit that he came in the name of the Lord.

The version *blessed is he who comes in the name of the Lord* is said to be a quotation from Psalm 118 verse 26, " with a slight change". The original, according to the Hebrew, runs, *blessed in the name of the Lord is he who comes*. The change in the order of the words is indeed slight, but the meaning is completely altered. A recent distinguished commentator[1] sees no Messianic reference in the verse of Ps. 118 in question. The psalm is a processional hymn sung by the people on their way to the Temple on the occasion of the paschal feast to thank the Lord (Yahweh) for deliverance from the bondage of Egypt and for victory over their enemies in the conquest of Canaan. The blessing of the priest (v. 26) immediately follows the sacrifice. He blesses *in the Lord's name* those who have come into the Temple, while the next

---

[1] E. J. Kissane, *The Book of Psalms* II, p. 219.

verse runs *we bless you from the house of the Lord*—that is, those who entered the Temple are blessed, and those of Israel outside are also blessed.

In the Septuagint, the Greek version of the Old Testament, the word Lord (κύριος) is always used to translate Yahweh, the name by which the Jews venerated God in all his power and majesty. St. Paul says the conditions of salvation are, to believe in one's heart that Christ rose from the dead and to confess with one's lips that Jesus is Lord (Ros. 10:9). Then he quotes the prophet Joel (3 : 32): *Every one who calls on the name of the Lord* (ὄνομα κυρίου) *will be saved.* St. Paul is here applying to Christ the words Joel used of Yahweh, words which would be familiar to a Jewish audience. Christ is coming with the name or title of Lord, and whoever invokes that name will be saved. The title was assumed by Christ himself in his preparation for the triumphant entry, *say the Lord hath need of them.* After washing his disciples' feet he said, *You hail me as the Master and the Lord, and you are right, that is what I am* (Jn. 13 : 13).

The title Lord had been given to Christ on cardinal occasions by way of confessing his divinity: After the Annunciation, Elizabeth under the influence of the Holy Spirit said, *whence is this to me that the Mother of my Lord comes to visit me?* (Lk. 1 : 43). The angels bringing the good news to the shepherds of Bethlehem said, *this day in the city of David a Saviour has been born for you, the Lord Christ himself* (Lk. 2 : 11). On the morning of the Resurrection the angel said to the women, *he is not here; he has risen ... come and see the place where the Lord was buried* (Mt. 28 : 6).

On the occasion of the Nativity the angels sang *glory to God in the highest* (Lk. 2 : 14). It is probably more than a coincidence that on the occasion of the triumphant entry to Jerusalem the crowds of believers sang the same refrain (Mt. 21 : 9; Mk. 11 : 16; Lk. 19 : 38) thus linking in memory, the public entry of Christ into his inheritance as Lord and King and his public recognition as Messias, with the day of his coming into the world. The first great act of the drama ends on a note of triumph.

The formula of acclaim with which the crowds of believers hailed Christ's entry into Jerusalem occurs again, this time coming from the lips of Christ himself in his final message to the Scribes and Pharisees: *Jerusalem, Jerusalem, thou that killest the prophets and stonest them that are sent to thee, how often would I have gathered together thy children, as the hen doth gather her chicks under her wings, and thou wouldst not. Behold, your home shall be left to you, desolate, for I say to you, you shall not see me henceforth until you say: Blessed is he that cometh with the title of Lord* (traditionally rendered *in the name of the Lord*) (Mat. 23 : 37–39).

Some commentators see in this expression of Christ a hint of the destiny in store for Israel to which St. Paul refers in *Romans* 11 : 25. The context, however, seems to point to a quite opposite conclusion, namely that we have here Christ's final warning to the leaders of the nation, pending his second coming as judge of the nations of the earth. When challenged at his trial by Caiphas, the high priest, *I adjure thee by the living God to tell us if thou art the Christ the Son of God, Jesus replied* [*Yes*], *thou hast said it. Moreover I tell you, you will see again the Son of Man seated at the right hand of power and coming in the clouds of heaven* (Mt. 26 : 64). This was a warning to Caiphas and his court that they would in turn be arraigned before the tribunal of Christ in judgement. Similarly he warns finally the Scribes and Pharisees, the official leaders of Israel, of the doom that awaits them. St. Matthew XXIII is a terrible indictment of their crimes.

Woe to you Scribes and Pharisees, you hypocrites, that shut the door of the kingdom of heaven in men's faces. You will neither enter yourselves nor let others enter. In sentence after sentence they are denounced as hypocrites. They *encompass sea and land to make a single proselyte, and then make the proselyte twice as worthy of damnation as themselves . . . blind leaders they have forgotten the weightier commandments of the law . . . they strain out the gnat and swallow the camel . . . scour the outside of the cup . . . whitened sepulchres . . . within full of dead men's bones and rottenness . . . serpents, brood of vipers, how can you escape the judgement of hell?* The day of mercy is past for the leaders of Israel. They are *vessels of wrath made ready for destruction.* (Ros. 9 : 22).

On his second coming to judge the nations of the earth Christ's credentials, so to speak, will be identical with those of his triumphant entry into Jerusalem on Palm Sunday. Then he came to assume possession of the throne of his father David with the titles of King and Lord. He was acclaimed by his followers who believed in him with the salutation: *Blessed is he who comes as King with the title of Lord* (Lk. 19 : 38). On his second coming he will be *seated on the throne of his glory, and all the nations will be gathered in his presence . . . and the King will say to those on his right hand, Come you blessed of my Father possess the Kingdom prepared for you . . . for I was hungry and you gave me to eat . . . Whereupon the just will answer, Lord, when was it that we saw thee hungry and gave thee to eat? . . . And the King will answer them, Amen I say to you when you did it to the least of my brethren . . . Then he will say to those on his left hand, Depart from me you cursed into everlasting fire . . . for I was hungry and you gave me not to eat . . . Whereupon they will say, Lord, when was it that we saw thee hungry or thirsty . . . and did not minister to thee? And he will say to them, Amen I say to you when you refused it to the least of my brethren here, you refused it to me* (Mt. 25 : 31–46).

This is Christ's description of his second coming to judge the nations. He will be seated on his throne and will issue orders and dispense justice as King and Lord. All men, just and unjust alike, will address him as Lord, confessing his divinity. Judgement of the world is one of the divine prerogatives of the Saviour (*Ros.* 2 : 16). He will come in his own right with the title of Lord (ἐν ὀνόματι κυρίου), exercising his supreme authority as Messias, that he formally assumed on taking possession of the throne of David.

Chapter Ten

IN ORDER THAT (ὅπως ἄν)

St. Luke 2 : 35

St. Paul *Romans* 3 : 4; *Acts* 3 : 19; 15 : 17.

"Purpose" is regularly and frequently expressed in Greek by ὅπως with the subjunctive mood. According to some grammarians ὅπως ἄν with the subjunctive is used very rarely and exceptionally to express "purpose." The instances, however, that are cited as exceptions will be found on closer examination not to be exceptions. It may be confidently stated that the ὅπως ἄν subjunctive clause never expresses "purpose" in Greek prose. The clause ὅπως ἄν with the subjunctive mood is always a modal clause, denoting the *manner* in which an action takes place, or the circumstances that control it; and is translated by "as", "according as", "howsoever", in such a way that, "after the manner in which", or by such other formula as will express the phase of modality indicated by the context; never by "in order that".

Plato

In *Phaedo* (59E) we are told that the prison attendants are releasing Socrates from his fetters and *passing him on instruction about his execution this day* (ὅπως ἄν τελευτήσῃ),—how he is to die.

Again, in the same Dialogue: *You must have courage and say it is my body you are burying, and you must bury it according as you wish* (ὅπως ἄν σοι φίλον ᾖ) *and in the manner you think* (ἤγῃ) *most fitting* (115E).

Similarly in *Gorgias* : A complaint has been made to Zeus by the panel of judges that men's lives cannot be fairly judged after their death on account of their knowing beforehand the date of their death. This foreknowledge had been given by Prometheus.

Now, word has been sent to Prometheus *how he is to deprive them of this privilege* (ὅπως ἂν παύση 523D)—that is, by enkindling in their breasts blind hopes of longer life.

St. Luke

In St. Luke (2 : 35) the prophet Simeon says to the Mother: *And thine own soul a sword shall pierce according as thoughts are revealed out of many hearts* (ὅπως ἂν ἀποκαλυφθῶσι . . . . διλογισμοὶ); that is, Simeon prophesies to the Mother the circumstances in which she will suffer: *according as* the designs of his enemies against her divine Son, from the immediate persecution of Herod until the Crucifixion, are unfolded.

Traditionally this ὅπως ἂν clause has been translated as a final clause: *in order that thoughts may be revealed out of many hearts.* The usual explanation of this version is that Mary's suffering is to show that men henceforth must take up their position for or against the divine Child, that there can be no neutrality. This certainly seems a far fetched interpretation. The rendering of ὅπως ἂν by "according as," is much more in harmony with the context. The revelation of thoughts or designs from many hearts will be the occasion or cause of Mary's sufferings not the effect or purpose. The divine purpose is to give the Mother a share with her Son in the work of Redemption,—*cum Christo compatiens.* The unfolding or revelation of the designs of his enemies against Christ will be, on every occasion, a sword at the Mother's heart.

St. Paul

In St. Paul *Romans* 3 : 4 a different phase of modality is expressed in the ὅπως ἂν clause. The Apostle has briefly referred to the great privilege granted the chosen people in being the recipients of the sacred writings containing the divine promises. Then the doubt is expressed, *can it be possible that, if certain people have proved unfaithful to God, their infidelity will neutralise God's fidelity to his promises?* St. Paul replies: *Impossible! God shall be proved true to his word, though every man be a liar, as it is written: howsoever* (ὅπως ἂν) *thou art tested in thy words, thou shalt also prevail when thou art judged.*

St. Paul quotes here the Septuagint form of the Psalm 51 : 6, the famous *miserere* psalm. It is usually rendered : *in order that thou mayest be found just in thy words and mayest triumph when thou art judged.* This version cannot be considered correct. No Greek writer of any period ever construed ὅπως ἄν with the subjunctive mood, to express "purpose", followed immediately in the same clause by a future indicative also governed by ὅπως ἄν— *that thou mayest be found just* (δικαιώθῃς) *and mayest triumph* (νικήσεις). A school boy would be corrected for such a construction. The Vulgate translator evidently suspected that there was something wrong. He rendered the future νικήσῃς by a subjunctive *vincas*. There is a reading νικήσῃς of inferior manuscript authority.

St. Paul, as I have said, is quoting the Septuagint form of the Psalm. Whatever may be the meaning of the original Hebrew form of this verse, the Greek as it stands in St. Paul *Romans* 3 : 4, means that no matter what scrutiny God has to undergo in connexion with his promises, he will emerge victorious out of the test. The verb δικαιόω is used in exactly this sense by Aeschylus describing a man *tested* (δικαιωθείς) like a metal for genuineness (Ag. 393). The proper rendering of this Greek verse is: *Howsoever thou art tested in thy words, thou shalt also prevail when thou art judged.* The context demands this rendering and Greek syntax also demands it.

Acts of the Apostles

In *Acts* 3 : 19 another phase of meaning is found. The context is the sermon of St. Peter after the cure of the crippled man at the Beautiful Gate of the Temple. After reminding the Jews that they had done to death the Author of life St. Peter now calls them to repentance. *Repent then and turn to the wiping out of your sins in view of* (ὅπως ἄν) *the coming of the day of consolation from the countenance of the Lord.* The clause is generally rendered here *in order that,*—the suggestion being that the repentance of the Jews would hasten the second coming of Christ. According to St. Paul *all Israel will find salvation when the tale of the gentile nations is complete* (Ros. 11 : 25). If the gentiles were being urged to repentance in order that the day of consolation for the Jews might come, this version would be intelligible. It is not suggested that the Jews themselves can do anything to hasten the coming of the day. As it is, the Jews are urged to repentance *in preparation for, against* (as the Knox version has it), *the coming of the day.* The phase of modality expressed in the ὅπως ἄν clause is the circumstance controlling the main action. The repentance of the Jews is urged *in view of* the coming of Christ. The attitude of Israel towards repentance is or should be, conditioned by this event.

In *Acts* 15 : 17 the ὅπως ἄν clause is again modal not final. The occasion is the Council of Jerusalem. Peter spoke in favour of admitting the gentiles to the Church without circumcision. *Then the whole company became silent and they listened to Barnabas and Paul describing all the signs and wonders God had performed among the gentiles by their means* (15 : 12). When they had finished speaking James took up the case: *Simon has told us how for the first time, God decreed to take from among the gentiles a people dedicated to his name. This is in agreement with the words of the prophet where it is written, Afterwards I will come back and build up anew the tabernacle of David that has fallen. Its ruins I will build up anew and will raise it up again according as* (ὅπως ἄν) *the rest of men seek out the Lord, even all the nations on whom my name has been invoked, saith the Lord making these things known from the beginning* (15 : 15-17).

James is interpreting the prophecy of Amos (9 : 11-12) that the Kingdom of David will be restored, as applying to the building up of the Church of Christ. The Davidic dynasty came to an end with the dethronement of Sedecias and his exile to Babylon in the year 587 B.C. The prophet Nathan had promised David that his throne would last for ever, *as long as the heavens, as the sun before me, as the moon that abides for ever* (Ps. 89 : 37-38). The literary prophets, Amos amongst them, related Nathan's prophecy to the Messias. In this descendant of David the prophecy would be fulfilled in the fullest sense. The angel Gabriel announcing to Mary that she would be the Mother of the Saviour said, *The Lord will give him the throne of David his father, and he will rule in the house of Jacob for ever, and of his Kingdom there will be no end* (Lk. 1 : 32-33).

The Church was not being built up *in order that* the rest of men would seek out the Lord. The *rest of men* means the nations outside of Israel, the gentiles who were being now baptised, *on whom God's name had been invoked.* It was of them that the Church was now being built, the Jews having for the most part refused to accept Christ. The rebuilding of David's tabernacle will take place *according as* (ὅπως ἄν) *the rest of men seek out the Lord*. The gentile nations are the material of which the tabernacle is being rebuilt. Israel will enter only when the building is complete (*Ros.* 11 : 25).

These are probably the only genuine instances of the ὅπως ἄν clause in the New Testament. Confusion sometimes occurs in manuscripts between ὅπως and ὅπως ἄν.